Partner Earth

partner Earth

A SPIRITUAL ECOLOGY

PAM MONTGOMERY

Destiny Books
Rochester, Vermont

Destiny Books
One Park Street
Rochester, Vermont 05767
www.gotoit.com

LIBRARY OF CONGRESS CATALOGING-IN-PUBLICATION DATA
Montgomery, Pam.
   Partner earth : a spiritual ecology / Pam Montgomery.
      p.   cm.
   Includes bibliographical references.
   ISBN 0-89281-741-0 (alk. paper)
   1. Ecology–Philosophy.   I. Title.
QH540.5.M65   1997   97-27281
577' .01–dc21   CIP

Printed and bound in Canada

10 9 8 7 6 5 4 3 2 1

Text design and layout by Sarah Albert
This book was typeset in Bembo with Gill Sans as the display typeface

Destiny Books is a division of Inner Traditions International

Distributed to the book trade in Canada by Publishers Group West
   (PGW), Toronto, Ontario
Distributed to the book trade in the United Kingdom by Deep Books,
   London
Distributed to the book trade in Australia by Millennium Books,
   Newtown, N.S.W.
Distributed to the book trade in New Zealand by Tandem Press,
   Auckland
Distributed to the book trade in South Africa by Alternative Books,
   Ferndale

To my Grandparents, Maxine and Forest Preston. Their loving example of stewardship of the land touched me at my core. Because of them my beauty path has led me to co-creative partnering with my beloved Partner Earth and all her beings.

CONTENTS

ACKNOWLEDGMENTS

I want to thank Amy for sharing with me through this long process while supporting me with good dinners, deep soulful love, and encouraging me to speak my truth. Thanks to my daughter, Cara, for her beautiful pen-and-ink drawings and her unconditional love. Thanks to my Mom for always being there; to my Dad for his desire that this book happen; to my sisters, P. Jaye and Patty, for sharing themselves with me (especially at Blacktail Ranch); my sons, Luke, Nick, and Chris, for the growth they have brought to me; and my darling granddaughter, Olivia, for helping me to become whole.

I want to thank Brooke Medicine Eagle and Rosemary Gladstar for their insightful, honest, and incredibly helpful comments, which brought this book to the next place. I want to thank my dear friends Kate Gilday, Andrea Butje, Deb Soule, Arti Roots Ross, Vicki Noble, Darryll Rudy, Indira Darst, and Gail Ulrich. Without their belief in me, this book wouldn't be what it is. Thanks to Gail Straub for all her prayers. Thanks to Sagewalker and Nadya Beck for helping me to know my true self.

A deep heartfelt thanks to Tag and Sandra Rittel, owners of Blacktail Ranch, for caretaking such a beautiful piece of Earth and making it available for others to enjoy. Thanks to Susun Weed for her inspiration and encouragement and to Eliot Cowan for his example.

I would also like to thank the many folks who contributed their stories or who inspired a story to be told. Thanks to past apprentices: Mary Dudek, Carol Douglass, Clare Wolf Song, Mary Brancato, Clare Buden, Caralyn Shapiro, Michele Leavitt, Gary Siegel, Lynwa McCartney, Deborah Caporrosa-Taber, Jane Phelps, Edie Locke, Cathy Parisi, and Rita Omark. Thanks to my Eagle Song sisters: Heron Wind, Marja deVries, Melanie Lohmann, Cricket Wingfield, Marion Gracey, Chris Ramos, Mary Buchsieb, and Linda Wass. Many thanks to other story contributors: Scott Montgomery, Zelaika Hepworth, Lois Hepworth, Amy Hepworth, Cara Montgomery, Luvia Jane Swanson, Hollis Melton, Cyndie Jansen, Kate Gilday, Andrea Butje, Marsha Green, Peggy Jackson, Jerielle Young, Sarah Morningstar, Robbie Lepzer, Deb Soule, Hart Brent, Debbie Nelson, Joyce Benedict, and Ian Blade.

I also want to thank my animal friends Chioya and Honeycat for their incredible devotion; my green friends, especially the flowers; the Hudson River; and the Medicine Rocks for the strength and guidance they have given me. Most of all I want to express my utmost gratitude to my closest of kin, Partner Earth.

FOREWORD

In this fine book, Pam Montgomery generously brings us with her as she steps forward into an entirely new realm of harmony with all our relations. I respect and honor her not only as a longtime close friend and staff member at my Eagle Song Camps, but also as my teacher; here she encourages us to achieve what we may perceive as too difficult or esoteric. Pam stands firmly grounded, with her head in the dawning starlight of a new day for all of us.

Some deep history of our planet may give perspective on the gifts that Pam offers. We two-leggeds pass through a new sign in the Zodiac approximately every month; Mother Earth passes through a new sign, or age, approximately every 2650 years. Many astrologers acknowledge January 23, 1997, as the beginning of the Aquarian Age on the basis of a specific star formation. History shows us that various kinds of energies and ways of being characterize each different age. The keynote of the Aquarian Age is global unity and communication, which lift us to a new plane of life.

In passing from the Piscean Age to the Aquarian Age, we pass from the time of the eight-pointed star to the time of the nine-pointed star. The philosophy of some native peoples says that the eight-pointed star is the star of the heart and refers to Venus. Our heart represents our emotional nature, and this nature allows us to bond peacefully with other beings and things.

During this past Piscean Age on Mother Earth, we have been growing in our ability to create conscious healthy relationship with all in the circle of life. Primary peoples have developed this to a fine and complex art with the surrounding creatures and plants that support their lives. In one way or the other, the vital issues concern the quality of our relationships. We are truly in the time of the heart and will continue to learn lessons about this for many years to come.

In this book Pam shares a route to healthy relationship with the circle of life. She has learned to respect, honor, and commune in a loving way with those around her, specifically her green-growing neighbors whose gifts offer extraordinary healing possibilities. Since many of us in this culture have not learned—or have forgotten—the importance of acting in this manner, Pam's lessons to us are of utmost importance if we are to live well (or live at all) with the others that make up this beautiful planet.

And there is more, for now, in addition to our overdue Piscean homework, we are assigned the lessons of the Aquarian Age, the time of the nine-pointed star in which the focus of energy moves up from the heart to the throat. This understanding corresponds not only to the astrological and native systems but also to the ancient East Indian chakra system.

The throat center contains creation and manifestation; all things earthly consist of vibration, so the voice represents our own creation center. Whatever vibration we embody with our entire being (not just our words) manifests in the physical realm. During this Aquarian Age, we must become conscious of our actual co-creation of life in concert with all that exists. As we come into this new age, we begin to understand how we create our own reality. This is our task for the next 2650 years.

Here again, Pam has stepped ahead of us, reminding us that we can no longer think of ourselves as dependent children whose conscientious mother will take care of us no matter how irresponsibly we act. She calls to us from the forefront of new thought, inviting us to begin thinking of ourselves in partnership with the great Lady Gaia, whom we have for so long called Mother. As we understand this next step in the evolution of our consciousness, we become able to put it into action and enthusiastically embrace our powerful ability to create life. In the recent past, we two-leggeds have been unconscious and negligent, if not downright dangerous and greedy. This has worked against what we need and want for our lives and those of our loved ones, as well as all the other beings on the planet.

Many prophetic texts tell us of our power to dominate all the other species on Lady Gaia. Now we can begin to understand that aspect of ourselves more fully, realizing that along with great power comes great responsibility, not only to ourselves but to seven generations of life to follow us. As we widen our perception, we see that in being dominant, we stand upon the backs of those below us as though at the utmost tip of an enormous tree. If we use our power to treat everything from root to trunk to flower with nourishing love and respect, the tree will be well and our perch secure. We now begin to see the deadly effects of not caring and not nurturing the life under us, as we find ourselves about to fall from the heights of a sick and dying tree.

Accepting our power and using it well, we can nurture the tree of life and all who live within it. Pam's pioneering work can make the path easier for all of us who follow. We can, and I believe we will, establish a path of beauty, harmony, and abundance on Gaia, our partner who returns love and nourishment to us in such bounty.

Brooke Medicine Eagle
Flathead Valley, Montana
Summer 1997

INTRODUCTION

We are on the verge of a massive leap in evolutionary consciousness on this Planet Earth. Not only the human species but all of life is participating in this leap. We have come to a critical juncture where either we evolve or we no longer remain on this planet as a sentient (conscious) species. Conscious participation—the use of all our awareness as thinking, feeling beings—is of the utmost importance for our current situation. The last century has clearly demonstrated a lack of feeling, and the thinking that has occurred is at best misguided. In this short span of time, we have managed to rape and plunder the resources of this beautiful Earth, leaving our future here in question. We have acted in the most unconscionable way by using our free will to dominate and destroy. We have taken the incredible gift of free will and used it to have power over all of life, thinking that we are in control or that we know what is best for others, both people and other life forms. Now we are faced with the consequences of our actions, and we must change our path of destruction and reenter the realm of sentience in order to continue as an integral part of this interconnected web of life. This is not a doomsday forecast but a deep realization from one soul of our misuse of will and how that misuse has affected all of life.

In order to fully comprehend the vastness of our task at hand, we must understand that we are not just a being with one little lifetime.

We are multidimensional beings with many lifetimes in many realms. All these lifetimes, with all of their thoughts and actions, affect the present, just as thoughts and actions today affect the future. We must also understand that all of life—defined as anything with a molecular structure and carrying a vibratory quality—is also affected by us and the vibrations we emit. We are a vast web of interconnected relationships, where every single thought and action is felt by all of the other pieces of the web. Each of us is a part of the whole, where no act is insignificant. We have a responsibility to the whole, Not only are we in relationship to all of life; we are actually a relative to all life. Everything in physical and nonphysical form that carries a vibratory quality is a relative of ours. Our very cells carry the memory of original creation, as do the cells of every other form of life. We are connected by origin, and that makes us all relatives. In order to be here in a conscious way, we must realize this at the deepest level of our being. Not only do we need to *realize* this reality but also to *participate* in it in an active way. To become fully conscious, we need more than just a relationship to all of life. We must become partners with life as we take the next step on our evolutionary spiral. We must develop equality, co-creativeness, co-reliance, trust, microscopic honesty, unconditional love, and communication. We must support all our relatives to be all they can be without jealousy, knowing that their success is our success; without fear, trusting that divine energy is guiding us all; without greed, realizing that this is truly an abundant universe where there is enough for all; and without a "power-over" attitude, understanding that true creativity comes from power within.

The journey to co-creativity is a process, just as all growth is, with challenges and shadow times. We can choose how to approach these challenges. I have chosen not to wallow in the pain and suffering (we seem to have plenty of that around us today) but instead to share my experience of the light. I do recognize that the shadow side is present and must be acknowledged and then released in order to let us shed more light.

What I offer is one woman's experience. It is here for those of you who are ready to hear it and for those who have had similar experiences and are looking for kindred spirits who realize that you're not alone or crazy. I am acting from my own authority and my partnership with all life. We all have the ability to operate from this place. It is our birthright. I share this experience with you in trust that it will be a homecoming, a resonance that strikes the chord of knowing, a remembering of all your ancestors (human and otherwise), and an evolutionary leap you are willing to take.

I

Journey to Co-creation

Living in co-creativity is an ever-changing, ongoing process. It is not an attempt to arrive but instead a conscious engagement in the journey. Many times within the co-creative process we must enter the "dark night of the soul," which is not a bad state, but the canal through which we birth our creativity. Knowing this place of darkness brings a depth of quality to the light that otherwise might go unrecognized. The co-creative process is about embracing both the dark and the light, trusting each turn on the spiral of life to be a conscious-raising opportunity. I share with you my journey to co-creation, its challenges and its gifts, sensing that my unfolding is not dissimilar from your own.

One of my earliest memories as a child was lying on the floor of our living room on a Sunday afternoon, with the sun streaming through the window, feeling warm and cozy. I was in that drifting place between waking and sleep where relaxation was so deep I wanted to stay there forever. Dad was reading the paper, and Mom was curled up on the couch with a book. I remember feeling so warm with my two parents, my heroes, near me. Life felt perfect in that moment. These were the two people I had chosen as my primary relationships in this life.

As a child I didn't always understand the challenges my parents presented me with. Now I can look at these challenges and see them either as areas of great pain and suffering or as part of a pact made between my parents and me that gave me an opportunity to grow and transform. I see, now, the great gifts that Mom and Dad gave me. I honor my parents and the contract I made with them in another reality. The recognition of this agreement has brought me to a deep commitment to fulfilling our pact for growth together. Some times are difficult, and there is still much healing work to do, but I view these difficulties through a wide-angle lens, taking into account the bigger picture. From this perspective, I accept our challenges together, knowing that they are helping me understand the richness of life.

The deep soul-nurturance of my childhood came from my grandparents on my mother's side of the family. As a young child I would spend time with them during the summer on their farm in the eastern hills of Kentucky. Granny and Grandad were wonderful "salt-of-the-earth" people. They were an extension of the land and knew no other way of life. They lived a simple country life, deriving pleasure from the song of a bird in the big apple tree in the front yard or from a blossoming rose in the side garden.

I remember that Granny was always in the kitchen, cooking something good. She spent a good portion of her day cooking, canning, or baking. The kitchen was alive with appetizing smells, whistles from the pressure cooker, and the twang of country-and-western music from the radio. When I arrived after long hours in the car, I would run to the kitchen, always to find a freshly baked cake sitting on the sideboard. I would lift the cake lid and take a big fingerful of icing. In midafternoon, after the main meal of dinner had been cleaned up, Granny would go out to her flower gardens. She had a green thumb and could grow anything. For the rest of the afternoon she would putter, prune, and pick. Sometimes I would hear her talking in a low voice as if someone were right in the bush she was working on. I'd ask, "Granny, who are you talking to?" She would simply say, "You know, plants are like people. They need friends, too." I wondered if her flowers grew with such vigor and beauty because she talked to them.

In the evening, I would curl up in her soft, round lap. She would kick off her shoes and take her first rest since sunrise. I loved the smell of her feet. To me it was the result of good honest work. On chilly evenings the coal stove would be fired up in the living room, and we'd warm our feet by it. When bedtime came, I'd go to my usual room and Granny and Grandad to theirs. Of course, I always had to get up in the night to go to the bathroom. Instead of having me go all the way downstairs through the living room and dining room to the bathroom, they would let me come to their room, where they had a chamber pot. I would quietly slip into their darkened room and hope that I didn't miss the pot.

In the mornings we rose early to the sound of the rooster crowing. Grandad and I would have breakfast together—a spread of eggs and bacon, biscuits and gravy, and fried apples or raspberries in cream. As we finished breakfast we could hear the train whistle in the distance. This was our signal to fetch the mail. In this early morning newness, the mist would roll down off the mountains and hover in the valley, with the shapes of the trees barely visible. We headed down the dirt lane toward the sound of the rumbling train. By the time we reached the train tracks, the mail bags were already being hoisted onto broad shoulders to be carried across the bridge to the general store on the other side of the river, where everyone went for their supplies. There was no car bridge; to get there we had to cross the river on a swinging footbridge. When we arrived, often a neighbor would be getting a haircut in the barber chair, or a young child would be trying on a pair of shoes in the dry goods section. Others were buying groceries or hardware supplies while waiting for mail call. When it was time for mail call, folks gathered around the small window, and the postmaster called out names. I'd wait with anticipation to hear Grandad's name. Then I would hear "Forest Preston," and my hand would wave wildly. Someone was writing to us—what news was this today? We then picked up Granny's baking supplies for the day, a box of BB pellets, and a plug of chewing tobacco for Grandad.

We often spent our day in the garden or in the fields. It was especially fun when Grandad would take Old Dick, the mule, from his pasture and harness him up to work in the fields. Grandad would let me ride him after putting his muzzle on—Old Dick loved to take bites out of little girls. Harvesting potatoes was another of my favorite jobs. Grandad would turn the soil with his digging fork, and I would unearth the little treasures. In such a short amount of time we'd have a basketful to bring to Granny.

M-m-m—mashed potatoes and gravy for dinner. After picking a mess of beans we'd make our way to the screened-in porch off the kitchen. Here Grandad would take a plug of Red Mule chewing tobbaco and stuff it in his cheek. Then we'd set ourselves to snapping beans. Once our chores were done we'd get out the BB gun and load it with our store-bought pellets. Grandad would set up a target for me under the big apple tree in the front yard, and I'd plug away at that target until my finger got sore. About then Granny would call us for dinner and we'd spend the next hour enjoying the fruits of our labor. After dinner Grandad would sit in his favorite chair in the living room reading a passage from the Bible. He never read silently to himself but always in a whisper. If I sat very still I could hear what he was reading.

The warm lazy afternoons found me under the papaw tree behind the smoke house. In the cool shade of the papaw tree I would hide away and let my fantasies abound. In the late afternoon Granny would emerge from the kitchen, bringing out tall glasses of lemonade. Grandad and I would sit under the apple tree sipping lemonade and doing math problems. He would say, "If you had two bushels of apples and on your way to market you picked up three more from your neighbor, but one fell off the cart from a rock in the road, how many would you have to sell?" I would take a stick and calculate the problem in the dirt.

One evening at dusk, Grandad and I were about to go in for supper when we heard a blood-curdling scream coming from the mountain. I ran and jumped into Grandad's lap, trembling from the frightful sound. Grandad assured me it was just the bobcats coming down from the high country to mate. I asked him why they screamed so loud, and he said, "Well, when you only have one chance a year to make a baby, you wanna get your partner's attention right away."

For our big outing of the month, we all dressed up in our fine clothes and went to church in a town on the other side of the mountain. Neither Granny or Grandad knew how to drive, so we would be picked up by a friend and driven to church. Church in the

South is no ordinary event that lasts only a couple of hours but is an all-day affair. Southern Baptists love to sing and praise the Lord in a very emotional and heartfelt way. I was always amazed that people would get up in the middle of the service and start praying and praising and preaching. It was so different from the very sedate Presbyterian services I was used to. These people were passionate about their faith and not afraid to express it. However, after a few hours the crinoline slip under my dress would begin to poke me everywhere. I couldn't wait to get that dress off and run and play. After church we would have dinner with Daisy Packard in her white house on the corner, with a picket fence and lace curtains in the window. I loved to go to her house. Something about being at her place stirred a deep memory for me, although I never could pull it to the surface. By the time we got home, everyone felt the fullness of the day. Grandad and I would slip into the kitchen and have a bowl of ice cream before bed.

Every day was filled with simple country ways, and yet a glorious wonder was infused in all that we did. With a compassion that ran deep, my grandparents instilled in me the knowledge that all living things have their place in the circle of life. Their love for the Earth and her abundance was the foundation for their daily walk. Their influence has directly affected the beauty-way path I've chosen. I am touched every day of my life by the teachings of my grandparents. My love and respect for Granny and Grandad is like the night sky—it knows no boundaries.

Grandad passed away while I was still in high school. I regret not having been able to spend any adult years with them so that cognitive knowledge could have been more embedded; yet I wouldn't trade the richness of my childhood experiences for anything. It didn't take long for my desire to be in the country to take hold.

While living in Baltimore and working every day in the city, I grew more and more anxious about the environmental crisis. It was in the early 1970s, and the Vietnam and Cambodian wars were now being overshadowed by the drastic issues of ozone depletion, cutting of vast tracts of forest, extinction of plant and animal species, environmental illness, and pollution of water and air. I felt an urgency for myself and the planet. I knew I had to learn to take care of myself and lead a saner, more Earth-based life. Friends in the southern part of New York encouraged me to move to this very rural area. I landed in Steuben County during the "back-to-the-land" movement and dove into country life with passion and purpose. I baked my own bread, formed a food co-op to order wholesome organic food at wholesale prices, grew a huge organic garden, and tapped maple trees for sap to make syrup.

During this time I met my future husband, Scott. He, too, was a lover of the Earth and was particularly interested in learning how to grow food and be self-sufficient. He and I decided to live on a subsistence level. We chose not to work at outside jobs but to live on the food we grew ourselves; the animals we raised for meat, eggs, and milk; and the plants we harvested from the wild. We heated our house with wood that we hauled and cut ourselves. We acquired the little money we needed by selling extra produce. We made a conscious effort to not overuse resources we had to pay for or that were not conducive to a balanced environment. I turned on the hot water heater once a week for family bath time or when Scott's mother visited. My stepsons, Luke and Nick, would dry themselves by the woodstove. We would all look squeaky clean and rosy like little cherubs.

Of course, these days had their challenges. "Living the good life," as Helen and Scott Nearing called it in their book by that name, also included hauling water from the creek after first breaking the ice with a sledge hammer. This was necessary because the water pump had cracked in two from the thirty-degrees-below-zero temperatures, and there were diapers to wash (we would never use disposable diapers). Then there was the time we closed off the whole house except the kitchen and dining room, where the woodstove was, because the wood supply was low and we couldn't get across the creek to haul more wood. The good times were great, and the hard times were—let's say—character-building.

The Steuben County days were very rich—I learned how to take care of my basic needs. I know that I will never starve. However, there is more to being nourished than just eating good food. My soul was crying for a deeper understanding of myself and my connection to the vast web of life. In answer to this plea, I became lifelong friends with another soul seeking the truth. Darryll opened the door wide for me to view the expansiveness of my being. I began to see the places in myself that were split and needed healing. I began to quiet myself and listen to the deep inner guidance. I began to know myself as a multidimensional being with more than one reality to explore. This shift in consciousness awakened my desire to know on an intimate level the very fabric of life, spirit, and all its manifestations.

Again, the universe heard my desire and gave me the gift of an amazing light being, who has become one of my greatest teachers. My daughter, Cara, was born in May 1981, on a clear spring day at the break of dawn. A symphony of birds welcomed her to this Earth walk. She is a very old soul, who has come to this Earth walk as a light worker to help humans move into this new age. I knew she had much to teach me the day she asked, "Mom, are there infinity grandmas?" I responded that I thought there were many grandmas. She asked, "But who was the first grandma?" I wished I could answer her questions but somehow never knew quite what to say. I told her I wasn't really sure who the first grandma was. There was a long pause, and then, with great conviction, she said, "I know who the first grandma was. Mother Earth." In that moment, I knew we had come together this time to do deep healing work with the Earth and all her beings. Cara continues to be an inspiration to me every day of my life.

There came a time when Scott and I realized we needed more in our lives than the daily hard work that came with subsistence-level living. We were grateful for the rich abundance of the land, but our souls were ready for a deepening of spirit. Scott has a gift of touch that I was always keenly aware of. I suggested to him that he take a massage class. He had to drive an hour and a half to Ithaca to class, but it was worth it. His creative center blossomed through massage. It was a vehicle for him to open to spirit and his knowing self. Once he had a taste of being in touch with his core being, there was no turning back. He decided to go to massage school. We sold farm equipment and scraped together the money for him to go to the Florida School of Massage. We spent the winter in Gainesville while he went to school. It was a deeply nourishing time for me. We had gotten together enough money so that I didn't have to work. I spent my days with two-year-old Cara, doing my own personal herb study and delving within. I knew that our days on the farm were over and it was time to move on.

After we returned from Gainesville, it was clear that Steuben County was not the place where either of us could pursue our heart's desire. We moved to Ithaca and found there an aliveness that nourished us. Then our time of growth together ended. Scott's heart went to another, leaving me like an empty vessel to be filled up. I filled myself with my love for the green world and my deep desire to participate in Partner Earth's healing.

My studies intensified when I enrolled in Empire State College, a school without walls where most work is independent study. I created my own curriculum, focused on holistic health education. My course work revolved around the study of energy and its movement through the body, artistic expression as a healing modality, discovery of self, and herbs. During this time I met Susun Weed, one of my mentors through Empire State, who has greatly influenced my life. She helped open my eyes to the different personalities of plants and the spirit that flows through them all. I spent hours talking with plants and getting to know them in an intimate way. This was the beginning of my love affair with the wild weeds.

I had taught myself much about herbs in the past, but now I plunged full force into learning everything I could. I became Susun's first live-in apprentice at her rocky Catskill Mountain homestead. My learning at Susun's homestead went far beyond becoming knowledgeable about plants. I spiraled into a world of the deep feminine—a world I had been only vaguely familiar with. Together Susun and I created the Wise Woman Center, a place for women to come and discover themselves. We invited notable teachers like Vicki Noble, Merlin Stone, Dhyani Ywahoo, and Brooke Medicine Eagle. It was a time of amazingly accelerated growth for me, when I discovered parts of myself I hadn't known existed. In our society, the feminine has been repressed; yet here I was in an environment where I could completely express myself as a woman in a woman's world. We were wild and passionate, strong and independent, sensitive and intuitive, emotionally expressive and accepting of our inner knowing. We created ritual to acknowledge the sacredness of all life, we danced in the light of the full moon, and we honored our grand-mothers who had walked before us. Earth, plants, animals, rocks, water, and moon came alive with our attention and desire to know them intimately. I came to know women as my sisters who walk a path of beauty supporting each other. During this time I met Amy.

Amy is one of the most unique individuals I've ever met. She has the biggest heart in the world and boundless energy to express her love of life. Being a double Pisces, she feels everything to the core of her being—which is sometimes a blessing and sometimes a burden. She not only feels within herself but takes on others' feelings. Because she is dedicated to experiencing joy in life, she wants others to experience it too. Amy spreads joy and good humor wherever she goes. She can talk and relate to anyone from anywhere, regardless of race, religion, or economic standing. She is also an Earth goddess, loving the Earth to a depth that most people don't even realize is possible. Being a seventh-generation farmer has enhanced her under-standing and experience with the earth. She has gone from being a Cornell graduate in pomology, with relatives who encouraged the use of chemicals in farming, to an avid organic grower who has worked diligently to bring an understanding of sustainable agricul-ture to the traditional farming community. This incredible woman took me by surprise. I had just come out of a ten-year relationship and was very intent on pursuing my herbal studies. The last thing I expected was to fall in love, especially with a woman.

Being in co-creative partnership with another human being is far more challenging to me than being in relationship to a plant. My relationship with Amy has been a true test of my ability to live co-creatively. I have found that the biggest weakness of humans (in-cluding myself) is the inability to communicate honestly. How ironic, since our level of communication is a distinguishing feature of our species. For the past eleven years, Amy and I have struggled to move away from defense into communication where true relat-ing can happen. We have learned through our process that the arena of co-creativity has infinite possibilities. However, placing ourselves in co-creativity instead of co-dependence has been like opening a door to the unknown. At times, it is quite frightening. The familiar is comforting even when it isn't healthy. Our relationship continues to grow, sometimes we take steps through the door of the unknown, allowing profound growth; other times we let the fear take over, causing immobility.

One thing has always been clear: our sincere commitment to Partner Earth. We have a mutual respect for each other's deep relationship to Partner Earth, even though our individual expressions of it have been very different. My spiritual connection has seemed rather far out to Amy, and yet her keen sensitivities feel what I'm talking about. When we first began our experiment with Devas on our seven-acre piece of land, Amy was full of questions: How were we going to work the land with beings we couldn't see?

My knowledge of Devas began when I read the Findhorn books and Dorothy Maclean's *To Hear the Angels Sing*. At that time I was rather young in my spiritual experience and didn't trust my own inner knowing. It seemed to me that I needed some kind of special psychic ability in order to communicate with Devas. Unfortunately, I did not possess this ability, so I left the communicating to more qualified individuals. Still, I had a burning desire to know more about these beings and their connection to humans. When I began my mentorship with Susun while at Empire State, she encouraged me to open lines of communication to these beings. She taught me to think and act in a nonlinear fashion, and that helped me expand my awareness of other realities. She also suggested that I get to know the individual personalities of the plants I was working with. I began by using close observation techniques and my five senses to experience the plants and relate to them as living unique beings. A journal entry from my experiences with Red Clover reads:

> While meditating with Red Clover, I had intense flashes from a previous lifetime. The whole feel of the morning was very familiar to me. I felt that I had done this exact same thing many times before. I remembered a time as an Indian when I was very familiar with the plants. A feeling of intense peace and calm was with me. I knew that this is where I find true peace and happiness—being intimately close with nature. I asked Clover to be my friend and to please tell me about herself. I held my hands over Clover in order to feel her life force. I focused on my chakras to see where her life force traveled to. I felt a heaviness between my third eye and

14

crown chakras. I tried to tune into my body to see where I felt Clover would be beneficial. My whole body tingled (meaning Clover is good all over or as a tonic, perhaps). What really is becoming apparent to me in working closely with plants is that each one has some very distinct feature that makes it different from any other plant. In looking at Red Clover what seems distinctive to me is the white patch in the middle of each leaf. It makes a chevron pattern. I'm not sure what this means. The flower buds are just beginning to come out. They are very hairy. They're almost like little paint brushes or brushes of some kind—cleansers? The back side of the leaf also has tiny little hairs on it. Red Clover has a very chlorophyll smell—lots of green. The taste of the leaf is not quite bitter, almost a little sour. There is a slight numbing effect on my tongue. My tongue also feels smooth and slippery. It seems that the leaf would be good for soothing raw areas by slightly numbing and smoothing and soothing. I got a very good feeling from Red Clover and felt that she was and continues to be an old and good friend . . .

I've been all consumed by Red Clover. I've been doing a painting for a long time that is inspired by taking Red Clover flower essence. I took the essence and two other people also took it. The main thing that came up for everyone was a feeling of balance, clarity, and added energy. For me, my heart chakra, which is the balance point in the body, totally opened. Today I sat with Clover and thanked her for the incredible opening she brought to me through my heart chakra. I asked her about her ability to heal cancer. She said that her ability to balance the body had a lot to do with it. I noticed the triune quality of her leaf. Perhaps this is another indication of her balancing affect. The trinity—body, mind, spirit; sun, moon, earth; maiden, mother, crone. Her flower is beginning to turn brown. She is definitely past her prime. Her flower has lost its subtle sweet taste, and her leaf looks a little mildewy. Ah, but she is by far still the sweetest most lovely flower of the meadow.

I then encountered an eye-opening book by Machaelle Small Wright, entitled *Behaving As If the God in All Life Mattered*. This book took all the mysteriousness out of Devic communication. Machaelle places Devas in the realm of everyday life and gives instruction on how to communicate with them easily and effectively. She offers a technique that uses kinesiology to communicate. No

Photograph by Pam Montgomery

deep trances or pronounced psychic abilities are needed, or even a belief in kinesiology. What a deal! Finally I had found a way to access the Devic realm without a lot of instruction and years of spiritual practice. I committed myself to having a garden that was a co-creation with the Devic realm.

On the spring equinox in 1989, Amy, Cara, and I dedicated ourselves to working in co-creative partnership with the Devas of our recently acquired land, where we intended to build our home and gardens. Our intention was to live as close to the land as possible and to infuse all of our actions and manifestations with spirit. We ceremoniously asked the Devas and nature spirits of the land to join us in this experiment. Shortly after this ceremony, a strange thing (or so I thought at the time) began to happen. In my peripheral vision I saw darting movement. This happened frequently, and often I would jump, thinking that someone was behind me. After about two weeks of this somewhat unnerving activity, I began to wonder whether it had anything to do with our ceremony asking the Devas to be in a partnership with us. I went back to our land, where I quieted myself and asked to be connected to the Deva of the land. Using the kinesiology techniques I had learned, I checked to make sure I was connected. Yes, I was. I asked whether the darting movement I'd been experiencing had anything to do with our forthcoming experiment. Before I could even begin to determine the answer through kinesiology, a rush of very excited energy surged through my body. I heard within my being a high trill of a voice that said, "Well, you said you wanted to do a garden and here we are. Where are you? Let's get started." It was such a resounding affirmation that I knew without a doubt that the Devas and nature spirits were there and wanted us to work and play together. I also realized from this first encounter that our connection was about action and manifestation, not idle information gathering. We were going to create together. After our equinox ceremony I was still sitting with my feet propped by the fire, waiting for the snows to melt, while the Devas were raring to go.

We planned the garden while it was still cold, then began our creation when the warm weather came. That spring we put up a tipi, which served as a home for three years until our house was built. It sat on a high bank, overlooking the Hudson River, where the rising sun greeted us every morning. The spiral garden, which we planted next to the tipi, became a constant companion. The outdoor kitchen that Amy built around an apple tree made me feel like the Swiss Family Robinson. I look back on those days of outdoor living and admit they were some of the best times of my life. There's nothing quite like waking to a symphony of birds, seeing the shimmer of the rising sun on water, and sipping early morning dew from the petals of flowers. The intimacy that we experienced with Partner Earth created a bond so unconditional that we know no separation between ourselves and her.

Since those early days, my partnership with the Devas has grown and expanded in ways that I couldn't begin to dream of on that snowy day in March. I have developed my own unique way of communicating that bypasses the more cumbersome and time-consuming kinesiology method. I have also moved beyond the garden arena and have incorporated Devas into every aspect of my life. They have guided me into an evolutionary spiral that is inspiring and enlightening and that holds promise for the future of this planet and all her beings. For this, I am eternally grateful.

2

EVOLVING THROUGH PARTNERING

EVOLUTIONARY SPIRALING

We are in the midst of a rapid evolutionary spiral where consciousness is about to make a massive leap. This evolutionary movement is not like any other, because it will not take millions of years to accomplish. This one operates outside of time and space, or rather, it controls the timing of itself. It is operating at an exceedingly high rate because of the urgency of Earth's plight. In the last decade we have experienced giant steps in self-awareness and spiritual understanding. Change is at hand, both within and without. Evolution itself is changing. The accepted idea of evolution as a linear progression from a lesser being to a more advanced life form is archaic next to the vast arena of co-creative consciousness. True evolution is the adherence of the individual's conscious intelligence to a primal knowing, and the changing understanding of evolution is that we can direct our own evolution. This is not achieved by thinking that we are better than other life forms or have dominion over them. Instead, we realize that we all arose from the same source and are of the same fiber. We can be humble in our sameness or oneness and at the same time give ourselves permission to be our own authority, not always looking for an external deity to direct our fate.

This process of evolution is really twofold. First, it is about remembering what we have forgotten. This, indeed, must come first, otherwise our creating or encoding constitutes only a superficial attempt. This primal knowing is awareness of divine energies, of which we all are a part. We must remember that there is no separation between this primal knowing and our own self-knowing. Healing this split is of crucial importance to us on our evolutionary path, for without such a healing we are unable to bring forth the natural elements of conscious intelligence that adhere to divine knowing. This remembering is about stripping off the layers of obscuration that we have placed on ourselves. It is a recognition that we are related to all of life and that our memory is linked to the memories of the animals, plants, rocks, water, air, earth, and all vibratory aspects of life. We are kin to all, yet we left home long ago and are only now beginning to feel a longing for home. This deep stirring within us is the first step to peeling the layers of obscuration, the veils that shield the light. We sometimes refer to this obscured part of ourselves as the shadow, or the dark self. This place inside ourselves is not "bad"; it is only where the light has been layered over or obscured. We begin our journey home by getting to know the shadow and little by little peeling away the veils to let the light shine through, thus fully partnering with self. Here lies the critical first step of evolution. To skip over this step and attempt to evolve by imposing a layer of multicolored light on top of obscured light is futile. This is one of the major complaints about the New Age movement. Ultimately, superficial patching makes the separation only greater.

Evolutionary movement is knowing that there is no separation between our conscious intelligence and divine energy. Conscious intelligence is not only an intellectual knowing but a knowing through the thinking mind, the feeling heart, and the multidimensional soul. Divine energy is the source of all creation, which lives in all beings and vibratory qualities. This is the common thread that joins us all as different manifestations of the same life force. We are evolving by reclaiming our birthright of direct relationship to all beings and by remembering that we are all from the same family with the same ancestors and the same roots of origin. Through this remembering we co-creatively evolve with our relatives by becoming partners with them. Together we move on the evolutionary spiral, knowing that we are all equal yet each carrying our own unique gifts to share with each other.

The memory that has mostly been forgotten is stored in the DNA of our cells. The genes that carry the hereditary codes are our ancestral memory. We haven't lost this memory; it is still there, but in fragments instead of whole pieces—or strands of DNA. Memory is not physical matter but vibratory filaments of light. Ultimately, our DNA is filaments of vibrating light that carry our ancestral memory. At present we have two intact strands of DNA that spiral around each other. Fully enlightened humans have the capacity to have thirteen strands (actually, there are twelve spiraling strands that all together make a unified thirteenth strand). The thirteenth strand is the creator connection. All the fragments of these DNA strands are available to us. Our task is to bring them back into alignment, to remember them. In other words, we must take all the members or pieces or genes or fragments of light and put them back together again. As Partner Earth and its beings have been fragmented, so has our DNA been fragmented. We are but a microcosmic reflection of the macrocosm.

Our desire to return home brings us to this place of healing the split with our relatives, which will heal the splits in our DNA. We must begin by recognizing all our relatives that have been abused, misused, overused, oppressed, and destroyed. This was begun through the environmental movement. However, it is not enough to lament the rapid cutting of the rainforest and the extinction of species of plants and animals, or to wonder about 65-degree weather in the Northeast in mid-January. What is needed is a sincere return to our relatives, where true healing can take place. We must listen to what they have to say and respond with genuine love and a desire to heal our grievous mistake of forgetting them, of treating them like mere strangers. This healing begins by asking them to renew our kinship through becoming partners. So we spiral around on our evolutionary path by expanding our relationship into one of equal co-creative partnership, where we work and play together to bring peace, harmony, and balanced manifestation to this planet. As we ask for this partnership we begin to remember what it is like to be a sister to the tree and flower, to be a brother to the mountain and river, to be a cousin to the bear and bee, to be a daughter to the stars and moon, to be a son to the wind and flame, to be Earth's lover. From this family foundation, this kinship with all of life, we remember our blood connection. We taste in our tears the salt of the ocean; hemoglobin and chlorophyll have similar molecular structure with only one different atom; the calcium of our bones comes from the very rocks we walk upon. From this deep knowing springs a new relationship, a solid partnering in which we strive for each to be all that it can be. We commit to this deep union of partnership, knowing that through deep commitment comes true freedom.

Healing the split between ourselves, primal knowing, and all our relatives is the first step toward becoming fully co-creative humans. Through partnering with all of life we begin to realize a state of constant creativity and a constant receptivity of divine energies. In this lies the second stage of evolution. In this state of grace we become increasingly clear about the creative process and the reality we desire to live in. On a cellular level, our DNA has pieces that are not encoded with hereditary material or memory. Scientists refer to this as junk DNA, since they don't really have any idea what its purpose is. We as co-creative humans have the ability to encode this DNA with whatever we choose. We infuse these light strands with the vibrations of love, peace, balance, harmony, abundance, equality, honesty, and joy. We no longer need to oppress people who are different; we no longer need to go to war; we no longer need to exterminate species of animals and plants; we no longer need to deplete the forests of the world; we no longer need to go hungry or be ravaged by disease, because we have chosen for ourselves an evolution that embraces all of life and brings forth a way to be on this planet that is vitally creative instead of destructive.

EARTH CHANGES

Earth has been experiencing changes periodically for its entire 4.6-billion-year existence. Every now and then, a rapid shift seems to be necessary, as happened with the sudden disappearance of the dinosaurs some 65 million years ago. When faced with seemingly drastic changes in climate like those we're experiencing now, we ask ourselves, "Is this the *big* change on the planet that causes life to change as we know it? Will we, too, suddenly disappear like the dinosaurs?" The changes we are now experiencing seem to be Earth's way of adapting to our industrialized lifestyle. Al Gore states in his book *Earth in the Balance* that "humankind is now changing the climate of the entire globe to a degree far greater—and faster—than anything that has occurred in human history."

Earth's participation in this rapid evolutionary spiral shows up in many ways, most notably in extremes of weather. The September 1993 issue of *Life* magazine ran a cover story entitled "The Year of Killer Weather: Why Has Nature Gone Mad?" The article states, "The three most damaging climactic disasters in U.S. history happened in the past twelve months." These "disasters" included Hurricane Andrew, the March blizzard that paralyzed the East coast, and the flooding of the Midwest. Then 1994 brought one of the coldest and snowiest winters I can remember in the East, and in 1995 the sixty-five-degree days in mid-January inspired me to barbecue. What's the message here? What is the Earth trying to tell us? Elbert Friday of the U.S. Weather Bureau says, "Taken together, the storms do make one wonder if there are pattern shifts occurring in our climate."

It is clear that Partner Earth has been jolted out of balance by our careless exploitation of natural resources, the addition of destructive chemicals, and our incessant warring attitude. Earth changes are in direct proportion to this senseless exploitation.

Machaelle Small Wright explains these Earth changes from an energetic perspective. For centuries humans took only what was provided for them from the wildlife and plants. They treated animals and plants as relatives, using only what they needed and honoring the life they shared. When humans stopped foraging and hunting to sustain themselves, they began to manipulate nature. Once seeds were put into the ground, the energy shifted from merely taking what was provided to taking what was desired. Slowly a change in consciousness began to emerge. A sense of control of the environment was being planted within as the seed was planted without. For a long time this control was not a "power over" but a creative power from within. The seed sower honored the seed, the rains that nourished the plants, the sun that filled the plants with vitality, and the soil that brought forth the fruit. When the harvest came, a ceremony was conducted to bless the abundance and to thank the spirit of the land that so willingly gave of itself. So, for many centuries the human input was gradually accommodated on an energetic level, and these changes were like a gentle wave of repatterning.

With the coming of the Industrial Revolution, this gentle repatterning began to change. With more and more people populating the earth, the illusion was created that there was not enough for everyone, that we must grow more food to feed the masses no matter what the expense. During the last one hundred years alone, centuries of honoring Partner Earth deteriorated into destructive dominion and greed. What is now seen by some as progress is merely a feeble attempt at security. This short-sighted "security" is clearly perpetuated by those who do not see themselves as multidimensional souls, as beings of light that partner with life, as divine energy. With the addition of so many new inputs in such a short time, the energetic repatterning has increased drastically. We no longer experience a gentle wave motion as the changes occur, but instead a violent shaking as Partner Earth struggles to rebalance the energy. This expresses itself in many ways, including the dramatic weather we are now experiencing.

We can clearly see our reflection in Partner Earth. What we do to nature we do to ourselves. Our nervous systems are experiencing the energetic shifting as an electrical short circuit. The fuses are being blown. We are chronically fatigued, stressed to the max, oversensitive, and burnt out. As we continue to deplete natural resources, our immune systems continue to malfunction. The largest organ in our body, our skin, is the major guardian of our well-being on a physical level. The more we cut, scrape, and gouge the skin of Partner Earth through bulldozing and paving Partner Earth, cutting trees, and mining, the more our immune systems are overworked in an attempt to heal the wounds. As we continue to deplete the ozone layer we are like the virus that pierces the cell wall to replicate itself. With the protective cell wall (ozone) punctured, the ultraviolet rays enter the atmosphere and alter the energetic balance, just as the virus enters the cell wall and shifts the biological balance. The addition of synthetic chemicals to the environment has caused an imbalance of the natural predator–prey relationship, thus creating an overabundance of certain types of bugs, fungi, and weeds that are seen as bad or detrimental to the successful growth of the crop. These seemingly "bad" invaders then take over, stimulating more chemicals to counteract them. This vicious circle results in a loss of diversity, the beginning of the downfall of a species.

Looking within, we see the increased use of preservatives, dyes, and synthetic additives in our devitalized foods. Are they the robbers of our natural internal predators, which scan the body for free radicals and keep the overdevelopment of these cancer-causing agents in check? As we continue to mine uranium from Partner Earth her heart weakens. We fill her arteries with toxic waste and garbage by polluting her waters, and heart attack becomes the number one cause of death. The microcosm reflects the macrocosm. As you do unto others, so will you do to yourself. Every action has a reaction. If we watch how Partner Earth heals herself, we may begin to understand our own healing process.

Partner Earth is healing her own split with humans through Earth changes which express her desire to change her relationship with humans. She no longer wants a parent–child relationship. She has been Mother Earth for as long as we know. She has sustained and nurtured us as only the mother of all can do. But the time of separation, when a child leaves its parent, has been with us for some time now. During this time of separation we have acted like a true adolescent—we know it all. Now the time of irrational experimentation is over. It's time to grow up. We can choose to move into a co-dependent relationship, wherein we take what we can get without regard for all of life, we use our relatives for our own personal gain, and we perpetuate our own obscuration, or we can move into a co-creative partnership, wherein we encourage the other to be all it can be, to look to the seventh generation ahead before we act, to shine our light on all. Choosing the former will lead us further into chaos, ending most certainly in our extinction as a species. Our only real choice is to move into co-creative partnership.

A partner is a player on the same team, two beings dancing together, an ally. The members of a truly co-creative partnership are equal; they create together to bring about balanced manifestation.

Partnership is about the union of form and spirit. It's about freedom through total commitment. Moving into this arena of co-creative partnership with all of life is a conscious act.

We choose to partner with the trees, thus coming to know them as the lungs of the planet. Through our partnership we realize that each breath we take is the trees' exhalation, and each of our exhalations is the trees' inhalation, and every single second of every minute of every hour of every day we exchange breath with this green world. We live in this constant cycle of exchange of oxygen and carbon dioxide. When we step outside the door in the morning and take a moment to share this breath in a conscious way, our vibration resonates with that of the tree. We move into a place of oneness where we acknowledge our tree relative, where we shine our light. This ray of light beams out and touches other relatives with a big YES! It is an affirmation that oneness and peace are here and now.

Our partnering with all of life must begin at a fundamental level: with ourselves, yet remembering that we are a part of the whole and that the whole changes when we are no longer consciously a part of it. We are integrally connected to the whole, so in speaking about ourselves we also speak about the whole, and vice versa. The more we integrate the whole as a partner, the more we partner with ourselves. I suggest that we begin through the power of words and change the way we refer to Earth. We are no longer a child to Earth. We are now becoming an equal co-creative partner. Earth is tired of being our mother—our adolescent period has worn her thin. She, too, is ready to evolve beyond the parent–child relationship. She is crying for a true partner, and so we answer her in wholeheartedness. She now becomes Partner Earth instead of Mother Earth. This may seem blasphemous to some, most notably the indigenous peoples who have never abused their mother. The Earth has always been our mother; how dare I suggest anything else. One friend said, "We'll have to change all our songs." We don't need to change the songs that came before; we can create new ones. I intend no disrespect. I merely long for us all to mend the hoop, to enter the full family circle again. Changing our relationship doesn't mean obliterating what came before—quite the contrary. It's important to embrace our childhood experience and learn from it instead of denying it. Earth will always be our mother but we can evolve into an expanded way of relating. Our relationship matures into co-creative partnership.

This time of change is both very old and brand new. We are reclaiming our birthright and coming home, but we are coming home to a brand new relationship. What an exciting time to be alive! For those who can envision themselves as multidimensional beings of light who partner with all of life, there is no doomsday vision but instead a vision of peace, harmony, and oneness. We wake to a brilliant sunrise with rays of radiant red and orange light flooding the sky. We give thanks for this beautiful day. We step outside to greet the new dawn, breathing in the green breath of the trees and plants. The birds sing us a good-morning song, and the wind gently caresses our face. We stroll through the garden, stopping to chat with our friends the flowers along the way. Our hearts open wide and are filled with the perfection of the moment. We smile as the joy radiates in and out. Is this a fantasy vision that exists only in the mind, or is it the potential held in the cells of each human being? If we can imagine it, it can exist, for our thoughts carry powerful vibrations.

Our partnering journey begins when we look at our acquired negative thought processes. We tend to view ourselves as not good enough; thus, our internal message is not one of peace but of war. We war with ourselves about how we look, how we act, how we don't act, how we could be more or better. We extend this warring attitude to our physical beings and see any imbalance or illness as an enemy that must be conquered instead of an ally that serves as a point of transformation. We war with our families through control and manipulation instead of making peace through cooperation and letting go. We war with the environment by senselessly taking without asking. Even the sustainable agriculture movement perpetuates the warring attitude by killing insects with organic and usually harmless substances. That form of death may be a little more benign for the environment at large, but it still carries the attitude, "How dare those bugs eat my broccoli?" We, the almighty humans, make war with life instead of partnering with the broccoli and bugs to see how we can co-exist together in a peaceful way.

During these times of change, growth is rapid because it must be. All of our thoughts, words, and actions are magnified. The more we carry war in our vibrations, the more the destruction and chaos increases. The more we carry peace in our vibrations, the more we experience light, clarity, truth, harmony, balance, and oneness. Free will allows us choice. Which do you choose? The time to live your truth is now. You would not be reading this book if you didn't know somewhere in your being that change is absolutely necessary. As actors in this magnificent play of life we have been rehearsing quite a while for this very time. Don't let yourself be swept away by stage fright as the curtain goes up. Let the star that you are shine and embrace your birthright as a co-creative being of light.

3

ASPECTS OF PARTNERING

HEALING THE SPLIT

The first step in co-creative partnering is to heal the split in ourselves, with our human relatives, and with our earth relatives. When we begin to truly partner, we find a caring that goes beyond relationship. The beginning of partnering is desire or longing. Desire to not be separate, longing to come home. Of course, it's much easier to partner with a person, animal, place, rock, river, or plant that we really like. The real question is this: How do we partner with a raging river that is about to flood our home, or a person who has taken advantage of us or who carries a different belief system, an animal that could attack us, a plant that is poisonous or gives us a rash or takes over our garden? Herein lies the challenge of partnering. How do we begin to see that these parts of life are relatives of ours that we have become separated from? We recognize them as family members and look for the part of them that is beautiful, even though it may seem very minute to us. There is a gift in each being, each encounter, each situation, each challenge. Unfortunately, because of our limited view of life we can't always see the gift or the place of beauty. As we begin to realize more of our multidimensional selves, we will be able to see beyond the microcosmic encounter that we are involved in and see the bigger picture that makes the gift in each situation apparent.

I was presented with an opportunity to heal a very big split one winter when I had a poison ivy rash all over the side of my face. As a kid I was often covered with poison ivy rashes. I walked around coated in pink calamine lotion. Poison ivy and I just couldn't seem to get along. A few winters ago we were burning wood that had poison ivy vines on it. It never occurred to me that I could get a poison ivy rash in the winter, so when a horrendous rash appeared on the side of my face I had no idea that it was poison ivy. I kept putting salves on it, and it just kept spreading. It progressed to the point where the whole side of my face was covered in crusty oozing blisters. Since it was on my face, I was "faced" with it every morning in an inescapable way. One day, at my daughter's school, a little girl came up to me and said, "How come you have pizza all over your face?" At that, I decided this problem needed to resolve itself. I went home and stared at myself in the mirror. In a flash I realized that this was poison ivy, and I vowed in that moment that I would change my relationship to poison ivy. That spring I observed poison ivy closely and listened to what the plant had to say. I began to recognize the gift that poison ivy has to offer us. It grows mostly where the land has been abused at some time. In my case, I live where there used to be orchards that were heavily sprayed with chemicals. Poison ivy is there to protect the land and help it recover from the trauma that was caused by the application of will. I began to have a profound respect for poison ivy and an understanding of the great service it gives to the land. The reality, of course, is that I still need to be in and among poison ivy because I harvest herbs in spots where it grows. I began that spring to eat three tiny red leaves once a day for five days. This helped my body match its resonance with that of poison ivy, and now I may only get a trace of the rash on my wrists. Every spring, as I eat my three red leaves for five days, I thank poison ivy for the wondrous gift it gives to us all, not just to the land— for when the land heals, we heal. This experience was *my* way of healing *my* split with poison ivy. (Please be clear that I'm not advising you to run out and eat poison ivy.)

Looking for the beauty and gift in all things is only superficial if we can't see these qualities in ourselves. All healing starts with self. There has been an increase in self-awareness and personal growth in the last decade. Therapy is now seen as an acceptable form of personal growth, whereas only a short while ago people who went to a psychotherapist were considered to be mentally disturbed or to have something "wrong" with them. This movement to know the deeper parts of ourselves, the hidden places, is clearly a movement toward healing the split in ourselves. It represents a longing to know the light beings that we truly are. To reach the light we must peel off the layers of obscuration, the veils that shadow the light. Through this process we come to know those shadow places intimately, recognizing that these parts of ourselves are not the enemy but merely points of transformation. This healing of the split is an integral first step in our evolutionary process.

During a recent intensive workshop, where the focus was specifically on entering into partnership with the devic realm, we began by releasing old patterns and realizing that if we wanted to heal the split with all our relatives we really needed to begin with ourselves. We each picked one area of our lives to work on that we felt no longer served us. We connected with the Deva of healing and with each person's higher self, or Devic aspect, as well as the Deva as the Hudson River, who served as our witness and reminder of the ever-changing flow of life. As each person spoke, I received an image of what that person needed to continue with the healing process. One particularly powerful experience was with Mary.

Mary wanted to let go of control. She felt that her constant need to control everything kept her from experiencing life to its fullest. She had been abused as a child and did not trust other people or the unknown. Fear ruled most of her life. To compensate, she rigidly controlled her surroundings, her feelings, and her relationships. She said that she felt as if she were an island unto herself and could never ask anyone for help. We began our work, and Mary started to cry as the fear crept in. I assured her that we all loved her and were there to support her fully to be all that she could be. I asked her to trust me. I told her to get on top of the picnic table and imagine that it was her island, where she was all alone. As soon as she was on the table, she curled up into a fetal position. I told her that she needn't be afraid because we were there for her, and that it took far more energy to hold onto control than to let it go. She had brought her blanket with her that day, and the rest of us took her blanket and held it firmly by the corners and sides. I asked her to jump from her island into the blanket, completely letting go of fear, control, and mistrust. As Mary stood at the edge of the table crying and trembling, we all encouraged her and told her she could do it. With a loud cry she jumped into the blanket. We bounced her in the blanket and rolled her around as she laughed and laughed. Peeling away another layer, she began to cry hysterically, seeing in that moment of freedom her deep longing to return home to herself and all her relatives. We gently lowered her to the ground and asked her for an affirmation with which to fill the now empty cup. She replied, "I am safe, I am loved, I am always loved." We chanted this affirmation to her several times so that it would lodge itself into her being.

We ended that time by acknowledging the support the Hudson River had lent us in our work, giving thanks for the reminder to be in the flow of life and to not resist change. We were also reminded to let go of what no longer serves us. We sang this song to the river and each other:

> *I take delight in the peace of a river flowing so gently*
> *to the strength of the sea,*
> *and I take delight in the love that is flowing just like a river*
> *between you and me.*

This experience moved us all. Mary's courage in letting go touched each of us in the places where we needed to let go. Her letting go was our letting go, so that we were all able to peel a layer of obscuration away and move closer to the light of our beings.

The flower children of the sixties felt a longing to return home, and they responded to it by using mind-altering drugs to glimpse the light; by rejecting the status quo and rebelling against authority, thus claiming inner authority; and experiencing freedom through sexual expression. The intentions of the flower children were noble but adolescent, because they skipped over the vital step of healing the split. The early stages of the New Age movement consequently became a bandage on a much deeper wound. We now are beginning to see the necessity of cleaning the wound and allowing it to heal from the inside out instead of superficially imposing high ideals in the hope of change. The New Age, by the way, is not a fad that will pass with time. We are indeed entering a new age. The difference now is that we are relating to it in a more mature way.

Once we heal the split with our biological family, other healings become much easier. However, if we skip over our primary relationships we will continue to be faced with similar challenges throughout our lives. We choose our parents and siblings while still in spirit form, thus making them our original connecting link to all our other relatives. Healing the split in these relations marks the beginning point of healing all our splits, since they are the ones during this lifetime that are primary. For many of us, healing may come through forgiveness. When we are small, we look to our parents as if they are gods, and when they make mistakes we are deeply shocked, hurt, and angered. At that time, we fail to see that they are striving to heal their own splits.

As a teenager I was always independent, and this trait carried over into my adulthood during the late sixties and early seventies, when everything under the sun was being experimented with. My mom, being from a Puritan-ethic background, didn't always understand my search to find a different way. Consequently, we weren't close while I was growing up, and we also didn't talk about our problems with each other. Only when I was in my thirties did things begin to shift for us. The birth of my daughter Cara was one of the most important events in my life. I wanted my mom to share in this miraculous happening, but she never came to visit me and her new granddaughter. Cara was two years old by the time they met. When I took her to see my mom, I had been so deeply hurt that I was catapulted into being microscopically honest. I told my mom all the things throughout the years that had hurt me, and she did the same. Even though these discussions were painful, they provided the opening that we had needed for so many years. For several years we dealt with the hurts between us, and gradually we began to see each other as two people with things in common that we actually want to share with each other.

At one point, my mom shared with me her sense of what had happened between her and her mother. My mother was the seventh child, and her oldest brother was nineteen years older. Three weeks before she was born, he died of typhoid fever from drinking out of a stream while on a hunting trip. My grandmother was deep in grief when my mom was born, and they never really had the chance to bond. So my mom began her life never feeling the close nurturance that only a mother can give. When she told me this story, a deep compassion rose up inside me. I saw clearly the split that she had carried with her. I saw how she had not perceived bonding with Cara as a monumental event, since her first message, as an infant, was not one of close bonding. In that moment of understanding I was able to forgive her. Forgiveness brings such freedom. I had carried this heavy weight for so long, and now I could let it go. My being became so much lighter. I had peeled away another layer of obscuration. I now involve myself in my mom's life as much as I can, living two thousand miles away, by calling her often, visiting, and going on vacations together. My heart has opened to her, and the more I open the more she opens. We can now disagree, maintaining respect for each other's opinions and knowing that we love each other very much. The healing of this split has been a big step in my evolution toward a being of light.

Perhaps if we heal the split with our biological parents we will then be able to heal the split with our earthly mother. Taking this evolutionary step will bring us to the place where we see our children as equals to be given the respect any human being deserves, instead of as lesser beings who need to be shown the way. Our children will no longer need to rebel, knowing that they are indeed creative powerful beings, just as worthy of recognition as anyone. As children of the Earth we begin to see the absurdity of carrying anger, fear, and hostility. Our adolescent rebellion can become instead a revolution, or more precisely a re-evolution. Through the process of healing our splits, we move into equality with the earth as we do with our parents and children. We become co-creative equal partners with all our biological, earthly, and cosmic relatives.

SELF-LOVE

An important aspect of partnering is being able to love ourselves, for when we can't love ourselves it's very difficult to love another. How do we begin to love ourselves when most of us were conditioned from the day we were born to not love ourselves? In my generation, most babies were spanked the minute they came out of the womb. What was the message? That the first encounter with physical life was violent and non-nurturing, and provided the beginnings of self-hatred, self-doubt, and low self-esteem. We are bombarded by family, society, and the environment with the message that we are not to trust anyone, including ourselves. Can't trust your sister because she'll tell on you, can't trust society because it will not provide for you (never enough), can't trust the environment because it will storm on the day you want to go to the beach. So here we are, wanting to create a different reality for ourselves without solid building blocks.

To begin this journey of self-love, we can start very simply by nourishing ourselves. Most people who are working to change themselves begin by changing their diet. This is an obvious attempt to nourish oneself more fully on a physical level. Nourishment happens not only on the physical level but on the emotional, mental, and spiritual levels as well. To fully love ourselves we must nourish ourselves on all these levels, not just one. Emotional nourishment has to do with feeling good, mental nourishment has to do with positive thoughts, and spiritual nourishment has to do with following our soul's path. We begin to nourish ourselves by surrounding ourselves with things we like and that make us feel good—in other words, things that have good vibrations. We all know the difference between good feelings and bad feelings. Good feelings are usually associated with joy, contentment, peace, and general well-being. Bad feelings are usually accompanied by a tight knot in the gut, uptightness, depression, and anger or fear. Keeping in mind that all of life carries vibration with it, we feel which vibrations make us feel good and which make us feel bad. Distinctly different vibrations are experienced from a walk in the woods and a walk on Fifth Avenue in New York. Some people may be completely nourished by Fifth Avenue, whereas others become very nervous and uptight in that setting.

To understand fully how nourishment works, we must look at the basic physical nature of our being. Susun Weed offers us a simple explanation. Basic life on a physical level is about replication and maintenance of cells. In order for cells to replicate, the DNA, which currently is a double helix spiral (two strands wrapped around each other) must unspiral. The DNA unspirals through vibration. This means that everything you surround yourself with literally goes into making up who you are. The vibrations that surround you cause the unspiraling of the DNA that replicates your cells. So if you are married to someone you don't really like, or you work at a job you don't believe in, or your workplace is uncomfortable, or you live somewhere you don't want to be, or you eat food that makes you ill, you are replicating your cells with vibrations that don't nourish you—ultimately, you are not loving yourself. Love yourself today by doing what makes you feel good, what excites you, what makes you happy. It's really quite simple: surround yourself with good vibes and you will know self-love. You say to me, "But I can't quit my job. I have kids and responsibilities." I understand this position and acknowledge that the journey to self-love may be a slow, painful process of letting go. Begin one step at a time, or perhaps introduce nourishing elements into your work environment. When you nourish yourself you nourish all of life, and this output and input of love has an effect. Placing yourself in this vibrational frequency of love can only serve you. The frequency of the love vibration is one of the highest frequencies, where major healing takes place.

We have the ability to choose love even in the face of despair. I recall the story of a prisoner of Auschwitz who survived the deplorable conditions there by immersing himself in the elements of nature. He would notice a bird flying overhead and become the bird floating on the breeze; he would hear the sound of water running and become the drop of rain flowing to the sea; he would feel the sun on his face and let the heat travel to his core, kindling his vital force. He chose to love himself so profoundly and live life so fully that the dance of death surrounding him was unable to touch him.

My own journey to self-love began when I moved from the city to the country. I had been living in Baltimore and working in an office. Every day I would take the bus to work in the concrete jungle. At lunch time I would go outside and walk blocks just to find the sun or a piece of green. I craved the grass under my feet and a way of life that was more meaningful. I wanted to breathe fresh air instead of exhaust fumes. Luckily, this need to nourish myself with an environment that I liked was realized at an early age. Moving to the country was a springboard for furthering the love affair with myself. My diet radically changed once I could have my own garden and grow fresh food. I kicked my Coca-Cola habit and began eating whole grains, vegetables, and fruit. What we couldn't grow ourselves we got from the co-op. We even raised our own animals for meat, until one day, after butchering a pig, we looked at each other and decided eating meat was not worth what we had just experienced. Since then I've been vegetarian. My journey to self-love took another big leap when I realized that working at jobs just for the money was not nourishing me. For some time I had been working the land and studying the wild herbs. I love the green world so much and am always happiest when I'm with it. One day I became aware that the best thing I could do for myself and the rest of the world was to make my passion my livelihood. At that point I committed myself to my herbal work and began building an herbal product business and teaching others about herbs. I have continued to make choices throughout my life that nourish me knowing that when I love myself in this way I affect all I come in contact with by carrying the vibration of nourishing love. Loving myself is the first step in loving other people, plants, animals, and all my relatives.

Throughout the summer, women came to apprentice with me and learn about healing herbs. One day before the arrival of some of these women, I decided to pick the wild greens for our salads myself instead of having someone else do it. For much too long, I had been involved in a project that had kept me indoors. I needed to get outside and touch the earth and the green beings. As I was picking lamb's-quarters and nibbling at the same time, I felt an overwhelming sense of love for these common little weeds. I saw in that moment how my picking them was nourishing me, and yet, at the same time, it was a profound act of love for my apprentices to lovingly pick greens with them in mind. Not only would these greens nourish their bodies with live absorbable vitamins and minerals, but the love vibration I was sharing with the plants would nourish the apprentices at the deepest level of their beings. Nourishing myself extended beyond me to those who ate the greens. Picking greens on a summer day—so simple and yet so profound.

My ongoing journey to loving myself is not always easy. I still remember my father's criticism; I still struggle with my addiction to coffee, knowing that it doesn't nourish my physical being; I wallow in victimization when my partner has an affair; I question my ability to recommend herbs, wondering whether I rely too heavily on my intuition. These issues are all very real for me. Yet, when I open my heart, I know that there is "no limit to the healing I ask for because the love source has no limitations" (*Direct Healing* by Paul Ellsworth).

TRUST

When we begin to love ourselves, the natural movement is toward trust. Trust is another important aspect of partnering. Without it there cannot be equality. Lack of trust sets up an atmosphere of doubt and constant questioning. It requires an enormous amount of energy to constantly wonder whether we are living in truth. Trust creates a deep knowing that sets us free from a tremendous energy drain and power leak. Trusting that all is exactly the way it needs to be is a very big leap in faith, especially in the face of disaster, disease, and deprivation. In order to trust, we must rise above our immediate concerns and glimpse the bigger picture, seeing how each action has an effect, and we must be willing to be microscopically honest.

Microscopic honesty is about telling the truth of our being down to the most infinitesimal piece. Not telling the truth is a huge obscuration we have layered on ourselves. We forgot the ability to communicate without speaking—telepathy—when we began to hide our truth. The few Earth-based cultures that are left, like the Masai tribe of Africa and the Australian Aborigines, still use telepathy as a form of communication. They have not separated from their source. They recognize themselves as part of spirit, as connected to Partner Earth, and as relatives to all beings. They have nothing to hide because they do not consider personal recognition an end in itself, and the voice of ego has not drowned out the voice of primal knowing. They see their place in the vast web of life as integral without losing sight of the rest of the web.

I think we hide our truth partly because we don't want to hurt others, however, we do not serve ourselves or others by not being truthful. We also can be truthful with compassion by realizing that we all come from the same source, our hurts are others' hurts, and their hurts are ours. When we allow ourselves to be microscopically honest with compassion, we come home to ourselves and the rest of our family. We are able to trust ourselves because we hear our first voice, the voice of primal knowing, more clearly. We are able to trust our relatives because they hide nothing from us as we hide nothing from them.

We must trust that our first voice, which comes from divine energies, is linked to the vast expanse of interconnected relationships. What is not always apparent to us in our microcosmic view of the world is known on the primal level. This means that even though we can't always see the bigger picture, we must trust that it is there, functioning in a balanced way, and that our thoughts and actions affect it. As we become more aware of our multidimensional selves we will realize that linear time is only one aspect of reality, and we will move into seeing the bigger picture and viewing the outcomes of our actions. This, of course, will happen when we truly become partners with all of life.

When we trust, we begin to see the gifts in each situation. We place ourselves in the river of trust and allow ourselves to go with the flow instead of creating friction by resisting. The other night my niece, Zelaika, was visiting for the evening. Her mom came to get her, and in the excitement of hellos and goodbyes she left without her book bag. It was a cold night, and I was happy inside my warm cozy house, where the fire was blazing. I noticed her book bag, and in order to catch her before she pulled out of the driveway, I had to run outside in my slippers without a coat. My response could have been one of non-trust, of negative resistance to going out in the cold to give her the book bag. Instead, once I was outside I noticed the incredible beauty of the night sky. The stars were blazing brightly in the clear crispness of the winter evening. I gave thanks for the gift of experiencing the beauty of the stars. If Zelaika hadn't left her book bag, I wouldn't have filled my being with the beauty of the night. The recognition of such beauty filled me with soulful nourishment. I happily gave the book bag to Zelaika, passing this vibration of beauty and nourishment to her. This may seem a very small act of

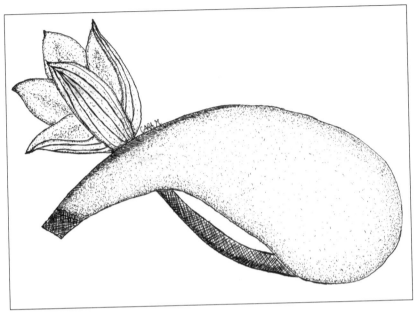

Illustration by Cara Montgomery

trust—yet, what would have been the consequence of not going with the flow? I could have not taken the book bag to her, thus missing the beautiful night sky and causing her to be in turmoil when she didn't have her books for school the next day. Or I could have grudgingly run out to give her the book bag without recognizing the gift of the stars, made myself miserable by the cold, and made her feel bad that she forgot the book bag. My trusting seems small, and yet, once set in motion, trust reverberates throughout the universe. It's like the pebble thrown in the pond that sends ripples to the edge. Trusting is an affirmation that life is unfolding exactly the way it needs to. It is a recognition that each seeming challenge is but an opportunity for growth and a point of transformation.

In order to trust fully we have to let go of the overwhelming desire to be in control. This has been a big issue for me, and I continue to be faced with opportunities to let go and trust. The first garden that I made in co-creative partnership with the Devas gave me one of my first big lessons in trust. I was told to plant twelve zucchini plants that year in my spiral garden. Now, all good gardeners know that you don't need twelve zucchini plants to feed a family of three. Four zucchini plants at the most are all that is necessary. I decided I would trust that these were the number of zucchini plants I needed to create a balanced energy pattern in my garden that particular year. That year we had steamed zucchini, zucchini bread, baked zucchini, sauteed zucchini, zucchini casserole, and everything else we could think of concocting with zucchini. All our friends and neighbors had zucchini, too, and we still had giant zucchini. On the farm where I live there is a large farm market stand. One day at the stand I overheard Lois, the owner of the farm, talking to someone about needing giant zucchini for one of her very good customers. Her customer needed large zucchini for zucchini boats. Of course, all good farmers harvest their zucchini when they are about eight inches long to ensure tenderness and succulence. Lois was upset because she had no idea where she was going to find zucchini this size—it's very important to her to accommodate her customers. When I overheard this discussion, I gasped out loud and said excitedly that I had several large zucchini suitable for making boats. This inspired me to visualize a whole chain of events that could have followed because I trusted enough to plant twelve zucchinis.

In my imagination, Lois immediately called her customer, Beth, and told her to come pick up her zucchini. Beth prepared a delicious zucchini boat dish for her party, where her friend Sheila tried and loved the dish so much that she asked for the recipe. Sheila decided to copy the recipe several times so she could give it to all her friends. While waiting to have her copies made, she began chatting with the clerk about the zucchini dish. Mrs. Bell, another customer in the store at the time, overheard the conversation about the dish. Mrs. Bell asked Sheila whether she could also have a copy of the recipe because she happened to be searching for a great zucchini recipe for the cookbook she was writing. Sheila said that first she would have to check with the friend who gave it to her, and then she would give Mrs. Bell a call. They exchanged phone numbers and parted ways.

I envisioned that Sheila immediately called Beth, who was very flattered and thrilled with the prospect of having one of her recipes in a cookbook. Sheila next contacted Mrs. Bell, and the two decided to make and eat the zucchini boat dish together. Sheila was looking forward to socializing because her husband, a diplomat, was gone for an extended length of time and she was feeling rather lonely.

The two women spent the day chatting and sharing stories. When it was time to eat, Mrs. Bell's housekeeper, Maria, joined them to give her opinion of the zucchini dish. Maria, a lively Peruvian woman and an excellent cook herself, was unusually quiet and seemed depressed. When asked what the matter was, Maria sobbed while explaining that her daughter was still in Peru and had been out of touch for months. Since Peru was on the verge of a civil war, Maria was worried that something awful had happened to her daughter. Sheila offered to contact her husband, the diplomat, who was in Peru right then. She thought that her husband might be able to find Maria's daughter.

Sheila called the American Embassy in Peru and spoke to her husband about Maria's daughter. The daughter turned out to be a companion of one of the leaders of the revolutionary forces. When she got word that her mother desperately needed to hear from her, she came out of hiding and went to the embassy to make contact. Sheila's husband was able to convince her to bring her boyfriend in to speak to him. She did, and through the efforts of embassy members, a peaceful agreement was reached between the opposing factions. Lives were saved, Maria was able to stop worrying, and Sheila's husband was able to return home. And although I dreamed up the conclusion to the story I knew it was all possible just because I trusted to plant twelve zucchini plants.

The simple act of trusting can have profound consequences. By trusting you place yourself within the flow of the river of divine energy that has far-reaching effects and moves the entire evolutionary process along. Trusting is a resounding "yes" that is felt on many levels. Not only is it felt when you enter the energy field of the garden, but the waves continue on and on, as we saw in the story of the zucchini boats.

COMMUNICATION

Communication is the aspect of partnering that most folks have a difficult time with. With the many layers of obscuration that occur, communication has taken on a new form or has become nonexistent. We have forgotten the art of truthful communication. We're unable to listen to ourselves or pay attention to synchronicity, calling it mere coincidence. We express ourselves through the logical avenue of the brain without regard for the feelings of the heart. We think we can only communicate verbally, thus eliminating the possibility of communication with the vast majority of creation.

I've come to realize that synchronicity is the life force trying to get our attention. We usually don't pay attention the first or second time something crosses our path, but the third time (third time's the charm) if we don't say, "Ah-ha, something's up here" we unfortunately miss our chance to be in that universal energy flow, and life becomes more haphazard. However, when we do pay attention we affirm our connection to all of life. As we vibrate at the same frequency as other beings we are riding the wave of corresponding resonance that creates a symphony when all our relatives participate. Paying attention to the synchronicity in life opens us up to real communication.

At one point, during the process of opening to the universal energies moving through me, I realized that I needed something more than massage to expand my physical ability to incorporate these new energies. My massage therapist friend, Andrea, suggested I investigate craniosacral work. I had heard of this bodywork before but didn't really know anything about it.

That summer I was in Montana working with Brooke Medicine Eagle and was gifted with a massage from the resident bodyworker. As we began the massage she asked me whether I would like some craniosacral work. I immediately remembered my conversation with Andrea and said, "Oh, yes." That session gave me one of the deepest bodywork experiences I've ever had. I knew that major channels were realigning and opening. Upon returning home it was on my mind to find a craniosacral bodyworker, but with my busy schedule I didn't take the time to find such a person. One morning I awoke from a deep sleep rather suddenly and sat up in bed. A very loud voice said, "You must have craniosacral work done." It was literally a wake-up call. Later that morning, Chrissy, my daughter's girlfriend, was dropped off at the house by her mother, Carol, to spend the day with Cara. As I was showing Carol around the house, she said she really needed to go because she was teaching a workshop that day. I asked her what the workshop was about. You guessed it—she was teaching craniosacral bodywork. I got my calendar out right then and made an appointment, and we have been working together ever since. Synchronicity seems to go hand in hand with intuition. In this situation I listened to my intuition, and the life force moved it along through synchronicity.

Intuition is our inherent ability to open to primal knowing. Because we have forgotten this vehicle of communication, it works in seemingly random ways. But when we consciously engage our intuition, we are able to communicate quite easily with all of our relatives. This conscious act immerses us in the current of life where true partnering can take place. It's conscious action that moves us beyond merely relating to the evolutionary step of partnering. Intuition is not necessarily a sixth sense but instead a full use of our five physical senses. Intuition is operating all the time—our problem is learning to listen to it. How many times have you said to yourself, "If I'd only listened to my intuition"? Just yesterday I was picking up a friend at the train station. We had agreed on a certain time when I was to pick her up. She called and left a message to remind me, but she gave a different time in the message. I knew that we had clearly specified a time—I had written it in my book. I also knew, because my intuition told me, that she wasn't coming an hour earlier. It occurred to me to call her and confirm the original time we had set, but instead I went an hour early to the train station and had to wait.

How much more efficient we could be with our energy resources if we listened to our intuition. When we take the time to quiet the constant internal chatter and release ourselves from the many distractions that society offers, we can hear that inner voice of primal knowing. If you think you don't have good intuitive ability, then practice listening.

Listening to our relatives is an important way to partner with them and heal the split that has occurred. By *relatives* I mean the elements, plants, rocks, animals, and all aspects of life. We ask our relatives, "Can you remember a time when humans didn't impose their will upon you? What do you remember about those times? What can we do together to bring about healing?" We then listen with humility, clarity, and light, which means with no judgment, with focused attention, and with radiant energy. During one of my morning quiet times, I communicated with uranium by asking to be connected to the Deva of Uranium. I asked what could be done to help heal the split with this powerful relative. Uranium replied, "I am the heart of Partner Earth, and I'm being ripped out of her. Bring Bleeding Heart flower essence and an essence made from flowers you find growing near me, and give them to me to heal this wound. My heartbeat is weakened. Drum to me to make my pulse stronger. Tell them to stop ripping me out of Partner Earth, or I will surely die." I began to weep as I listened to my relatives pleading to be heard by their brothers and sisters who had left them. "Please come home" is their plea. I hear loud and clear, "Tell them, dear soul, little sister, to return to the fold where we can all be as one family again." I began planning a homecoming healing at a uranium mine—which is difficult because these mines are not accessible to the public.

In listening to Uranium I realized that many are fearful of this powerful relative, but the fear comes from a lack of understanding of uranium's place in the design. Trying to control the immense strength of uranium has only made us more fearful. It's when I begin to look at the beauty of uranium, the creative essence, that I see how to partner with this formidable relative.

I find that when I appreciate the beauty of a person, place, plant, animal, stone, or idea I am much more open to communication. On the other hand, whenever I meet judgment of a critical nature, I shut down the channels of giving and receiving energy. Judgment perpetuates a warring attitude. Recognizing beauty is the doorway to the heart, and true communication is transmitted through the heart, not the head. Often I find myself bombarded with superficial thoughts as I'm attempting to communicate with my relatives. I take a moment to quiet myself, and to feel into my heart, and to visualize the heart chakra opening and clear channels of light radiating toward whatever it is I want to communicate with. When these channels are open, there is unobscured access to primal knowing. Partnering takes place when this conscious intelligence is recognized and listened to. Some may refer to this as "channeling." Everything is channeled when we are in partnership with life, and every human being has this capacity.

ot blindly give over our authority to an unseen
ceived as all-knowing. In a co-creative partnership
al standing with our partner.

_anneling isn't necessarily hearing voices that clearly instruct you about life. We can understand a lot by merely paying attention to our bodies, which carry conscious intelligence in the nucleus of every cell in the form of DNA. Because our cells are directly connected to spirit, we have at every given moment the ability to "hear" or know what spirit is saying. Our challenge is to focus on the message that is coming through our bodies. Eugene Gendlin describes a technique called focusing whereby we can get to the core of our body's inherent knowing. Gendlin uses this technique mostly in the psychological arena; however, its application is appropriate any time you're not clear about what your body is trying to tell you. Gendlin uses the term *felt sense* to refer to what is going on in your body, and the term *handle* for the word that clearly describes how your body feels. He asks you to check the felt sense with the handle by resonating with them both, back and forth, until you become totally clear.

I have worked with felt sense in many different ways. When I want to make a connection with a particular Deva or guide, I quiet myself and allow myself to move into a different frequency. What this feels like in my body is what I call elephantitis (not to be confused with the disease elephantiasis, which sounds similar). The term *elephantitis* is my handle for the way my body feels as if it were getting bigger and bigger. When this sensation first started to happen, I became alarmed by the way my body expanded further and further. Then I realized that I wasn't losing myself—I was only expanding my conscious awareness to encompass more of life. I've also had the sensation of everything becoming super-soft, as though I were surrounded by velvet. When I feel these sensations I know the channel is clear, or as if I have dialed up someone who has then picked up the phone. Felt senses are particularly useful in work with plants. Mary, an apprentice, was working with yarrow and felt a cooling sensation throughout her body. By listening to this felt sense, she was inspired to investigate the possible anti-inflammatory properties of yarrow, which she did in fact find.

One way in which we can tune into our relatives when we give our focused attention is resonance matching: operating on the same frequency as another relative. With people, we refer to "being on the same wavelength." Well, it's the same with any aspect of life. When we're on the same wavelength, communication is a given rather than a chore or something that requires effort. When we're on the same frequency, our bodies affirm this by giving us a felt sense that feels good. Good "vibes" are a great indicator that we're connecting. If we ever need a little assistance in reaching a particular frequency, sound is a great way to match resonances. Toning with the different chakras (the energy centers of the body) or using instruments like drums and rattles helps us to tune into our relatives. A tool I like to use is my crystal bowl, which is made from the same quartz crystal that is used inside radios. I make the sound by running a rubber-tipped mallet along the top edge. The sound is a high-pitched frequency that acts like a direct line to the star beings. Another commonly known use of sound is the *Om* chant, which is often used in meditation or as a means of focusing. *Om* is the sound the cosmos makes as it swirls through the heavens.

Another form of communication is more mechanical than those just discussed. It is known as kinesiology, or muscle testing. Machaelle Small Wright, in her book *Behaving As If the God in All Life Mattered,* demonstrates it as a technique for successfully communicating with Devas and nature spirits. Kinesiology works with electrical currents that run through our bodies, called meridians, and affect our muscles. There is a positive energy field, a negative energy field, and a ground wire. When we place ourselves in a positive energy field, our muscles become strengthened, and when we place ourselves in a negative energy field, our muscles become weakened. When we ask a question and the answer from the Deva we are addressing is positive or "yes," then our energy system reflects that positive energy field with strength, or an in-flow of energy. When the answer to our question is "no," we are in the presence of a negative energy field, which our bodies reflect through our muscles as weakened energy, or an out-flow of energy. Of course, for energy to flow uninterrupted, there needs to be a ground wire. A simple visualization of roots growing from the bottom of your feet into the earth can ground you. The breath can also be an effective grounding tool. It's important to remember that kinesiology is not a belief system but a basic law of nature, so true skeptics may find it more acceptable. Anyone who has been to a chiropractor has probably experienced kinesiology in the process of finding out which systems of the body are weak or what supplements will strengthen the body. This is how it works: if, when you raise your arm, it is strong enough to withstand downward pressure, then you are in a positive energy field or are strengthened. If your arm easily is pushed down, then you are in a negative energy field or are weakened. This form of kinesiology can be very cumbersome, since you need to rely on another person to assist you.

The technique Machaelle offers in her book is to make a circuit by connecting your thumb and little finger of your nondominant hand, then placing the forefinger and thumb of your other hand inside the circuit you have created with your thumb and little finger. Now ask a question. If the answer is yes, your fingers will stay together when you try to separate them by applying pressure with your forefinger and thumb. If the answer is no, your thumb and little finger will easily come apart. The third way of using kinesiology is quite simple. Place your hand over your hara which is the chakra or energy center just below your belly button. This is the energy center that connects you to the rest of the universe. When you are in a positive energy field there is a forward pull on your body. When you are in a negative energy field there is a backward push on your body. The movement can be very slight, so you must learn to detect very subtle energy movements. But it can also be so strong as to knock you off your feet. Kinesiology is a great place to begin communicating with your relatives. However, it can be very confining, since the questions you ask are limited to "yes" and "no" answers. It also can be time-consuming and tiresome. After an hour of asking questions, your little finger is mighty weary. What I have found is that it is an excellent tool for those whose intuitive abilities have lain dormant. It's like a jump start to the intuitive sense. You will find after some time that you will know the answer before you can even get your fingers into a circle.

Another form of mechanical communication is dowsing, or

divining. This is a technique of using a weighted object on the end of a chain or string and again asking questions. The pendulum will swing in one direction for no and another direction for yes. I imagine the word *divining* comes from the early understanding that we have access to divine knowing. There is an excellent exploration of divining in Sig Longren's book *The Pendulum Kit*.

The most important thing is to do what works for you. We are all unique individuals and have our own ways of communicating. There are no set rules and regulations. Old forms are falling away, and new ones are being created through our partnering. As we practice communicating with our relatives it becomes easier and easier. Then, at a certain point we move into that place where there is no separation, and our sharing becomes communion, for we know that we are in common union. We know that this place of common union is our birthright, for we all carry a piece of the original spark of creation within us.

PLAYFUL PARTNERING

In the many workshops I've taught about partnering and co-creation with the Devas, I've found that people want to "work" at this relationship. They get very worried that they are not doing something right or are not asking the right questions. The whole process becomes very serious. This surely is exactly how to hinder the partnering process. Devas and nature spirits, as well as Angels, are very light, playful beings. If you relate more to shamanic partnering, deep communication through shamanic journeying is a blissful experience. When we truly commit to partnering with all of life, we enter a state of grace that incorporates play, humor, happiness, bliss, and ecstasy. Think of all the times in your life when you have been happy. Most likely you were playing and purposefully having fun. You were probably with friends, with family, or in nature. You were choosing to be happy in that moment. One of the great awakeners to joy, Patch Adams, says, "The most revolutionary act anyone can commit is to be happy. I refer not to a moment of joy during one of life's peak experiences but to a basic pattern of enduring happiness. It takes no greater effort to be happy every day than to be miserable."

There seems to be an overriding belief that we can't be happy, that life is about pain and suffering except for fleeting moments of happiness. Is it possible that this belief has permeated society because of our separation from our source? Is it the loss of family connection, of the sense of being a part of the whole, that veils the light of happiness? When we feel our kinship with all of life we feel supported, nourished, and loved, all of which make a happy person. The fabric that the life force is made of is bliss. Deepak Chopra refers to bliss as the "vibration that bridges mind and matter." Basically, what he is saying is that bliss is the medium through which spirit infuses form. So when we are consciously partnering with life and co-creatively infusing form with spirit, we are swimming in a sea of bliss. Our task is to jump into the sea, roll in the waves, splash and laugh, and see that every moment is an opportunity to play in and with the divine essence of life.

The effects of joy are healing at the deepest level. It is a proven fact that humor, joy, and happiness stimulate the immune system, increase circulation and oxygenation, slow the aging process, and create a relaxation response. When we are happy our bodies secrete the chemicals endorphins, which give us energy and make us feel good. This is the vibration we carry in ourselves that nourishes us at the cellular level. It is also the vibration that is emitted. Happiness is infectious. When we are around happy people it is very difficult not to feel the effects of the happy vibrations. So how do we choose happiness in a world where greed and hate still flourish? We begin by allowing ourselves to have fun and play. We let go of control and spontaneously laugh. We appreciate the beauty and gifts in life that bring smiles to our hearts.

In Montana, one summer, I was teaching a group about flowers and making flower essences. We began our experience with Thistle by observing her and noticing how beautiful she was. I had my magnifying lens with me, so we all looked even closer at Thistle. We saw through the close-up view that Thistle's pollen was iridescent blue. This discovery sparked oohs and ahs, and before long we were anointing our faces with iridescent blue sparkles. We giggled and played with Thistle before we sat down to talk with her. This playful encounter was the opening door to partnering with Thistle.

On another occasion, I was with a friend on the small island of Vieques in the Caribbean. We happened on to a beach where the white sand bottom of the sea went out for hundreds of yards and the water was never deeper than chest height. The water was warmer than bath water and was the most incredible aqua color I've ever seen. I immersed myself in the water, bobbing and swirling and gleefully experiencing the warmth, the radiance of sun and sea, and the crystalline light dancing on the ocean floor. I played with the sparkles of light on the surface of the water and on the sand under the water. I watched as the light danced and skipped around me, then I danced and skipped with the light. I felt myself in an ecstatic state of aqualove. This experience has stayed with me at the deepest level. All I need to do is think of aqualove, and I'm there again feeling my cells being loved and nourished. I even bought an aqua rug for my living room to constantly remind me of aqualove. Joy, happiness, and playful bliss are around us all the time. We can choose them at any moment. Perhaps when we're ready to choose happiness, our world will become a peaceful place.

My partner, Amy, takes her joyful partnering experiences one step further and allows herself to enter into an ecstatic state of orgasmic bliss. While she feasts on the abundance of nature, her deep desire to merge with the profound beauty around her leads her into communion. Her common union with nature inspires her to open her chakras to the earth. She begins by dropping down to feeling the rhythmic undulations of the earth. She moves with the earth while at the same time breathing deeply into her *hara,* the center of her sexual expression. As the energy begins to rise from the earth she breathes it in. She rides the waves of blissful energy to the point of light explosions. As she floats in this sea of oneness an enormous sense of gratitude and sweet peace fills her. This love vibration radiates out, allowing this blissful experience to be felt by all she comes in contact with. It then becomes not her experience alone but is woven into the fabric of life. This experience is a deeply intimate one, which most people have only with a lover. Imagine being able to be lovers with all of creation!

4

WHAT IS A DEVA?

LUMELLIGENCE

My experience with the devic realm has been expansive and always enlightening. I have struggled with my own limited ideas about reality and what I perceive to be real or "only my imagination." Growing up in a society that places very little merit on imagination or anything in the unseen realms hasn't helped. However, when I'm connected I know without any doubt that intelligence is a part of all physical, emotional, and mental life. Many have referred to this intelligence as Devas or Angels. *Deva* is a Sanskrit word that means "being of light." G. A. Gaskell, in his *Dictionary of All Scriptures and Myths,* describes Devas as "Shining Ones." Dorothy Maclean, in her well-known work *To Hear the Angels Sing,* refers to Devas as "Builders of life who transmute energy into physical structures including emotional and mental." Machaelle Small Wright describes Devas as "an intelligent level of consciousness within nature that functions as the architects within all form." William Bloom, in his pamphlet entitled *Devas, Fairies, and Angels,* says that Devas are "architects that have the blueprint or design for manifestation." From these definitions you can see that Devas have to do with light, intelligence, and bringing into form. In my deep desire for understanding, I wonder how we get caught in terminology. I talk to many people about Devas, and many of them describe experiences that are clearly openings to the devic realm—yet they still don't trust. Is it the words themselves that limit us in our ability to understand the unseen realms? The term Angel has a particular meaning to those from a Christian background. Even though Angels are described in a similar manner as Devas, they are relegated to the arena of religion and don't necessarily play a part in the rest of life. In India, the understanding of Devas is quite common and extends somewhat beyond the realm of religion. Yet, even there, Devas are still confined to a limited arena. My experience with this vast luminous intelligence is that there are no limitations to when or where we can be in communication with it and make use of the deep knowing of how to energetically bring about manifestation in a balanced way.

In my struggle to communicate what I'm talking about, I have come up with a word that many may be able to relate to. *Lumelligence* combines the words *luminous* and *intelligence*—which is as close as I can come to describing what Devas are in our modern world, where religion and culture have become separated. By referring to Devas or Angels as Lumelligence, we bring them into a more universal dynamic, where all may experience their essence without getting hung up in the connotations presented by words that have a history. These changing times are all about old forms falling away and new ones emerging. Our vocabulary must change also if we are to become a global and universal family that strives to unite instead of separate.

Light Quality

I refer to Devas as Lumelligence because there is a distinctive light quality to their essence. Sometimes it can be seen as an egg-shaped ball of light, whereas at other times it's a different shading of light similar to that of a daytime eclipse. On still other occasions it may be seen as a vibrantly glistening light. Often it is perceived as fast movements or darting streaks of light. During an intensive workshop where our topic was devic partnership, we were weaving wreaths for our heads, and I was inspired to take pictures of the women as they wound flowers into crowns. When the pictures were developed, one showed an egg-shaped ball of light hovering above the heads of two of the women, Gabrielle and Sonia. This was the Deva

Photograph by Pam Montgomery

or Lumelligence of Green Terrestrial (our home), which was partnering with us as we prepared for our final ceremony together.

While on a vision quest in Montana, I sat against some rocks, known as the Medicine Rocks, looking at a mountain. These rocks were on the old Northwest Trail, which crossed the Continental Divide. It was common practice for the Native Americans, as they crossed the Divide to hunt buffalo, to stop at the rocks and offer prayers, since these rocks were known to hold healing powers. At the base of these rocks, surrounded by a patch of bearberry, I quested for a vision. At my back was a solid rock face, and in front of me was a sloping hillside that fell to a small valley where the north fork of the Dearborn River meandered. Across the valley, an ancient guardian mountain reached for the sky in what seemed to be a communion between heaven and earth. I offered my prayers and let myself move into the place of connection and communication with all my relatives. I asked for support in my vision so that I might clearly see my path. I realized in that moment that people throughout time have been asking for guidance from Lumelligence and that the shamanic tradition in indigenous cultures is one more way to connect and communicate with the intelligent light energy that exists everywhere. I returned to this same spot a year later and sat against the Medicine Rocks one more time. I acknowledged my tremendous gratitude for all that had been given to me during my vision time. On this occasion, I had my camera with me and took a picture of the mountain guardian that had been my constant companion throughout my quest. When the photo was developed, there on the mountainside was the light essence of the mountain shining through, affirming once more the presence of luminous intelligence.

Amy had an experience of light beings one day as she was working in the field. She was contemplating a particular problem with the production of vegetables. She asked quietly, within herself, how to deal with the problem. As she continued her work she noticed light beings before her that resembled handkerchiefs. When she focused on them she saw that they would rise in the air and then float to the ground as if one had thrown a handkerchief into the air. After acknowledging the light beings, the solution to the problem she was contemplating became clear to her.

In my early days of partnering with the devic realm, my first experience of their light essence was in my spiral garden. It was one of those soft magical days when all was right with the world. The sun shone down, warming me to the soles of my feet. The wind whispered the promise of the day in my ear while the birds encouraged harmony in their joyful song. I was alone in my garden, feeling a deep sense of satisfaction that after three years this garden was coming to a place of dynamic balance. In this state of grace, and in that moment, I knew what co-creative partnership is all about. It is creating balanced manifestation by infusing form with spirit. As this flash of re-membering was taking place, I looked up and saw a white figure standing in the garden. I gasped, and in an instant the figure was gone. I immediately began to explain away what I had seen. Oh, it was the edge of my white t-shirt, blowing in the breeze and catching my eye, or it was a sudden burst of dandelion fluff released into the air. My old mistrusting self was so quick to take over. I stopped in that moment and thought of the insight I had had just before the white figure appeared. No, I wouldn't let the old judgment take control. I did see a white figure in my garden. I dared to validate my own experience. Of course, it was time for me to understand the light essence on a deeper level by being shown the figure and to gain a profound lesson in trusting my own experience.

An acquaintance, Luvia, shared with me an experience of not only the light essence of Devas but also the oneness in which we all reside and the interconnectedness of humans with all of life.

> An experience of unity occurred for me when, sitting on a favorite riverbank, I felt the presence of a warm, loving, light being moving within the center of my body. I felt a lightening and expansion around my heart and solar plexus, and caught a brief glimpse of a female, robed figure. She responded to my questioning that she was "Sunlight on Water in the Forest." I was surprised that there would be such specificity of identity, then reflected on how I had experienced her within and through myself, as a part of myself. It occurred to me, with a sense of startled awakening, that a part of me is Deva, just as a part of me is Earth, and a part is human, and a part is extraterrestrial. This was an experiential, cellular knowing of how, indeed, we are all one. We experience identity in accordance with how and where we focus our consciousness, and we can, therefore, learn to shift our focus—or, in effect, tune the frequency of our consciousness to exist on various levels. For instance, in order to be able to communicate with Devas, we simply match frequencies with them, which usually means relaxing and expanding the mind to receive more subtle signals.

Intelligent Quality

Intelligence, according to the dictionary, is the ability to understand relationships and to communicate information and also is "the basic eternal quality of divine Mind." The example given of an intelligent being is an Angel. How is it that a plant knows exactly when to emerge out of the ground in the spring, or geese know when it's time to fly south, or the sun knows when to rise each and every day, or a rock knows how to slowly mineralize the soil? All of life carries a piece of divine mind, which gives the plant the ability to know that when the ground thaws and the moisture from the spring rains fill its seed full to the point of bursting, it is time to press against the soil all around it and seek the light of the sun to help it grow to maturity, when it can drop its seed again. The plant understands the relationship it has with the soil, the water, and the sun in order to fulfill its purpose in life. Communication takes place on many levels. A plant can communicate its need for water by drooping. A rose may communicate that one can look past the thorns in life for the beauty that lies beyond. Stinging nettle tells us to pay close attention by the pricks it gives us. We receive this communication through observation. What if we open ourselves to communication beyond what is obvious? We then move into the place of conscious relationship known as partnership.

During an exercise to gain information from plants through all of the senses, one of my apprentices, Clare, had an experience that illustrates the intelligence and high level of communication that is possible with Devas.

> I had one of my most powerful openings to the Devas when she [Pam] left me with an unknown plant to observe by myself. The first thing that I did was use my sight to observe the physical aspects of the plant. It was growing on the edge of a field by the woods. There was quite a bit of her, with companions such as dandelion, my chosen plant ally for the apprenticeship I had received through meditation in a previous class, as well as ground ivy, poison ivy, and violets. It was growing close to people, and I sensed it was a perennial. The plant was very green. This got me thinking about the heart chakra. The stalk was green with soft, white hairs. The leaves had five sections. This symbolized life for me, as I observe the sacred number five in the pentagram. The leaves were smooth, with a silvery underside, and there were quite a few of them. I inhaled her smell. I smelled the sun, flowers, incense. The smell went to my head, and I immediately sensed that this plant would bring psychic protection. It brought up memories of drumming, dancing, chanting, and full moon nights. These were from my soul, not my present memories. It was hairy and bitter in taste, so I felt this was not a plant for food. There was a chalky taste that reminded me that she has lots of minerals and salts. I decided that I needed to lie down on the Earth with part of her with me. I inhaled her scent as I drifted into trance. I felt that grounding and flow of energy from the Earth, and I relaxed contentedly on her body. I closed my eyes and felt as if I were dreaming. There was a

woman in green dressed in my plant—or was this my plant? It must be the Plant Deva. She was painting me with her leaves, and everywhere she touched me [I] became her. She was on my arms and chest and face. I was not alarmed, but I knew to go with the flow of energy to keep the relaxation. I decided to not try so hard. Immediately, I felt the energy go to my solar plexus and third eye, which brought up thoughts of the dreamtime and astral projection.

Then, I was in another place and time as I squatted and bled on the Earth, feeling extremely rooted and nourished. I decided to go see "The Old One Within" and ask for her guidance. I had been led to her before through a meditation journey in a previous class. As I came to her, she spoke to me but not in words. It was an understood communication through thoughts and feelings as well as sensations. These words seem inadequate, but there is no word to describe this communion. She "told" me that this is a nourishing plant that contains vital hormonal structures that are important for younger and older women. It is a plant used for dreaming in a moon lodge. This common but graceful plant is to be used in the changes of our life cycles. For me personally, I should use it with my plant ally, the dandelion, for my bleeding time. Then, the Old One placed a piece of the leaf in my womb and heart chakras to move their energies, to heal my blocks, to birth my creativity. Most importantly, I was initiated as a Woman Healer.

I came back slowly into this time and place and fully into my body. The rhythms of the energy were still swirling in spirals in my womb. I felt the physical and energetic presence of the leaves. I felt honored to learn directly from the Plant Deva and the 'Old One Within.' I grounded myself and let the excess energy go into the Earth. When I opened my eyes, the sun was warm and shining brightly on me. I could hardly wait to share the experience with the group. We all came together to share our learning from our observations. Pam told me that my plant was Mugwort and that she is known for psychic and dream work. She is a uterine tonic and is used in colds, flu, and coughs. She can be preserved as a vinegar or tincture and dried for a tea. The group was amazed by the connection I made, and I felt truly initiated as the Woman Healer I have always felt called to be. This is my path, and I am so grateful to have plants as my teachers along the road of life. This was the beginning of my work with plants for healing along with psychic and energetic healing. What a wonderful repository of information! The Devas seem to bridge the gap for me between physical bodily healing and the energetic patterns that support all life.

Clare's experience is clearly an example of communication with the intelligent essence of mugwort. Her channel of communication through the Old One Within was a way for her to involve her own devic aspect and participate in the communication process. She was able through relaxation to match her resonance with that of mugwort, thus the sense of becoming the plant. The ability to match resonance and move into the oneness is the most effective method of communication. In this space, there is no separation between you and your relative. The common union of being a part of "divine mind" that we all have is apparent, and communion takes place.

The universal resonance, frequency, or vibration that is always an open doorway to communication is the one of love. Unconditional love is the place where oneness lives. Marja, a quester at Eagle Song Camp where I've worked for a few years, sought to learn about pure unconditional love while on her vision quest. Her teaching came through the experience of oneness.

I became one with the grass. It felt lovely to wave in the wind. Being grass, I could feel the difference between being trampled down without even being noticed and being trampled down as an offering that I, as grass, was asked to bring as a humble contribution to the bigger whole of life. I felt that grass, too, loves to contribute, to be useful, and doesn't mind being trampled when there is pure intent. This feeling overwhelmed me. I was struck by the insight of how much willingness and love everyone and everything seemed to be ready to give as soon as they saw that, by doing so, they could serve the bigger whole of life.

Next I became a rock. I became not only the rock itself but also the aura of the stone. I wanted to know how it felt to be picked up as a stone. I discovered that if it just happened, it felt alarming. As stone, you are completely dependent upon the person who picks you up. It is unsettling if you don't know what the person is going to do with you. Maybe you will be suddenly thrown away or dropped. When it has been told to you, as stone, why you are picked up, then it is much less upsetting. When the intent for use for the bigger whole of life is explained to you, as stone, then the experience becomes a joyful one filled with love. This experience of oneness was new to me, but having now felt it, I know the truth of it.

Later, I asked to be connected to the Overlighting Deva of the area in which we were vision questing, which is known as Blacktail Ranch. I immediately heard a voice calling me, "Come, I will show you the river." While my body stayed under the tree, I went to the place where we had done our ritual bathing to purify ourselves for our vision quest. I was told, "The love of the river, as you experienced yesterday during your purification ritual, is there for everyone. The river doesn't make any discernment; she gives her water, her refreshment, her purification, her beauty to everyone." Then I was taken to a flower. It was a beautiful Spreading Fleabane, a tender little radiant white flower with a yellow heart. "Look," I was told. "This little flower is beaming with all of her beauty for everyone, like the stars. She, too, doesn't discriminate. She gives her beauty and love to everyone who passes by. Look at the tree you have chosen to sit under for two days and two nights. You have approached him respectfully. The tree likes that. But if you had not done so, the tree would still have given his love to you. If you had not made the effort to open yourself to the tree and be respectful, then you would not have felt the love from the tree. This is how it works. Do you know why the river, the flower, the tree, and everything in nature gives their love unconditionally? Because they are not afraid. If you don't know fear in your heart, you will be able to love everyone and everything. Fear blocks the experience of love.

Marja's clear intelligent communication from the Deva of Blacktail Ranch helped her to see the limitations created by carrying the vibration of fear and to see how the unconditional love vibration is the key that opens the door to the vastness of all of life.

One of my apprentices, Mary, relayed the message she received through her communication with the Deva of the Green Terrestrial spiral garden:

All around there is love. Love which has created your world, love which holds all things together. Your very world, everything you touch, stand upon, breathe, eat, is composed of love. When you begin to open to love, the universe is ready to receive you like a child being born again, surrounding you with tenderness, holding you with care. In opening to the universe, you let go of the smallness of self and you become part of the vastness of the entire universe—the ocean, the sky, the earth, animals, plant life, all that is.

MANIFESTATION

The third major aspect of the devic realm is that of bringing into form. This is where we can all begin to relate, since our existence here on this Earth is specifically in physical form. However, the Devas hold the energetic design for balanced manifestation not just in physical forms but also mental and emotional forms. We begin devic partnership when we recognize that all form is infused with spirit and that this spirit carries light intelligence—lumelligence.

A clear example of the manifestation process came while I was on vision quest in Montana. My site was about three miles from the base camp. Normally, questers are not permitted to go this far from camp, but when I first encountered the Medicine Rocks, I knew this was my spot. I told Brooke Medicine Eagle that this was where I wanted to quest. She said that it was too far away to be able to hold the energy and that she wanted me to stay within the bowl of Blacktail Ranch. I attempted to find another quest site, but nothing spoke to me. All I could see in my mind was the Medicine Rocks on the trail to the Continental Divide. Brooke, having known me for several years, was aware of my deep connection with the Earth and all her beings. She had much respect for my work with the Devas. As the day of the quest drew nearer I knew I had to go to the Rocks. I asked to be connected to the Deva of Blacktail and asked whether there was any other place where I could be and still receive exactly what I needed in this quest. The answer was "no." I asked the Deva of Blacktail to help me get to the Medicine Rocks for my quest. The next day, Brooke came to me and said she had discussed with Tag, the owner of Blacktail, the matter of my going out to the Rocks. He had agreed to let me go. The process of balanced manifestation through co-creative partnership had been set in motion merely by my asking. My internal fire rose as I began anticipating the two days and two nights of communion with all my relations.

As I hiked out the trail leading to the Medicine Rocks my heart soared when I heard the shrill cry of the high-flying hawk escorting me to my destination. Already, my relations were gathering to support me in my quest. The north fork of the Dearborn River criss-crossed its way through the valley. The cold water of this high

Photography by Pam Montgomery

mountain stream sent streaks of exhilaration all through my body, and I took deep heavy breaths of air. The oxygen burst in my lungs and quickly traveled to my head, where lights danced as I took in the pristine freshness of the moment. Flower-filled meadows rose on one side, and the stream meandered on the other. I stopped to rest for a moment, sitting among the lupine, Indian paintbrush, yarrow, and clover. The buzz of insects busily pollinating and drinking nectar filled the air. The gentle breeze kissed my cheek as I quietly observed the aliveness of the meadow. I laid my head next to a pinkish-purple clover blossom and looked closely at the hundreds of tiny spires that made up the blossom. I nuzzled the soft petals as the delicate fragrance seeped through my being. The scent teased me until my lips could no longer resist the sweet treasure stored in the waiting blossom. I took the petals into my mouth and for an instant knew the ecstasy that every bee in this meadow was experiencing. The squirt of nectar was the juice of the gods, surely.

I arrived at the Medicine Rocks at high noon. The spot I had picked for my circle included the south face of the Medicine Rocks;

a patch of uva ursi, also known as bearberry; and a small pine tree. Seated within my circle, I looked out on a grove of ponderosa pines that gently sloped down to an open meadow, where the north fork of the Dearborn River made its way from the Continental Divide to the valley below. Directly across from me was my guardian, an ancient solid mass of stone that held the secrets of the centuries. Here was where I would partner with all my relations and ask for a vision to guide me in my Beauty Way.

As I created the outline of my circle, where only energy that would serve me on my quest was to enter, I prayed to Great Spirit for guidance, clarity, and understanding. I spent my first day in quiet prayer, asking to be connected to all the relatives I was surrounded by. I sat most of the time in a patch of bearberry. This is a low-growing evergreen that produces berries that the bears love, hence its name. I'd never spent much time with bearberry before because it doesn't grow where I live. I asked that the Bearberry Deva share with me what I needed to know at this time. The day was fairly uneventful, with no great flashes of inspiration, and yet I felt a perking within me. It was as if something just below the surface were trying to emerge. As evening approached I prepared myself for night in the wilderness. I had no tent, only my sleeping bag and a tarp to protect me against inclement weather. I curled myself up in my sleeping bag, buried my head, listened to the sounds of the twilight, and worked to calm myself for the unknown of the night. Suddenly something began hitting at my sleeping bag. It was a sharp quick movement that penetrated my bag slightly. I lay very still, trying to imagine what might be doing this and working to quell my rising fear. Slowly, I peeked outside my sleeping bag. There in the fading light I saw a hummingbird. I went into a panic. All my life, I have carried a great fear of birds, especially when they come close to me. It stems from a past life in which I was a Native American who was staked out and left to die, and the birds pecked me to death. This fear is understandable but still uncontrollable. I begged the hummingbird to leave me alone. At my request it left, and I drifted into an uneasy sleep. I awoke to a symphony of birds and wondered how could I be so afraid of creatures that made such lovely music in perfect harmony. I watched the sun as it glided up the valley and greeted the day with a sun salutation. Again I asked to be connected to my relatives the rocks, the bearberry, and the mountain. I found myself investigating every nook and cranny of the Medicine Rocks. These rocks were where centuries of Native American peoples had offered their prayers and gifts. They hold a sacred energy that I have felt only on occasion. As I put my cheek next to the rocks, I heard, in a felt sense, the prayers of my ancestors who had come before me. Essentially the prayers were for a peaceful life. I asked the Deva of the Rocks to tell me what was I to do with these prayers. What I heard, not through my ears but through my heart, was that all these centuries of prayers were leading to a time in the very near future when peace would come to this planet. But before then, much change in Partner Earth and all her beings, especially human beings, would be needed. Humans have lost touch with their divine source, so that their change must be at the core of their beings. As the prayers of the rocks reverberated in me, I wondered what this profound change could be.

As the afternoon of the second day wore on, I sat with my back to the Rocks, looking at the mountain across from me. I noticed how formidable it was—so solid and present, and felt supported in my search for understanding and clarity. I asked to be connected to the Deva of the Mountain. The drowsiness brought on by the afternoon sun suddenly disappeared, and I was keenly aware of an awesome presence. Again, through my heart, I heard the mountain telling me to pay close attention and listen to all my relatives. The changes at hand were mighty, and I would need the strength of a mountain to follow through. I took this as a message to quiet myself and move into a meditative state, in which I could listen more closely to my relatives. I lay down in the patch of bearberry and began deep breathing to quiet my inner being. Again, I felt as if something were trying to emerge, like a seed breaking ground in the spring. I traveled inward and searched for the core of my being which was where this change was to take place. I went deeper and deeper on an inner voyage past limbs and organs and blood until I came to a spiraling strand of light. I was at the nucleus of my cells, the very DNA. I listened with every fiber of my being. Here was where evolutionary change occurred. This was the place where our light essence emerged from. I saw twelve strands of light in different colors, spiraling up through the center of my being, up out of the top of my head and then cascading down like a waterfall and back to the base of my spine again. I was dazzled by the light essence I experienced and felt a wholeness in my being that had never been there before. Feeling finally complete, I reveled in this awareness for quite some time and then gently dozed off.

I awoke as the sun was setting, and there in front of my eyes, perhaps three feet away, was the hummingbird hovering, seemingly motionless. I stiffened, letting the old fear creep in. Then, remembering the mountain and the advice to listen to my relatives, I calmed myself and asked to be connected to the Deva of the Hummingbird. I asked the hummingbird if she had anything to share with me. She said, speaking to me in my heart, "Don't be afraid to act on your visions even if they are seemingly far-out." I thanked her for this wise bit of advice, and she darted off. As twilight approached I readied my bed for the night. On my second night in the Rocky Mountain wilderness, I was much less apprehensive.

Some time in the middle of the night, I awoke to the brightly shining moon. Lying there, I was aware of how different the light of the moon was compared with the sun, which had been relentlessly shining for the past two days. By now I had learned to pay attention to every little thing that crossed my path. I asked to be connected to the Deva of the Moon and then invited her to share her message with me. She told me, through my heart, "My light can bring balance to this world. For many centuries our Earth has been ruled by the Sun Gods, and it is time for my aspects to shine forth. Through my light I offer feminine intuition, magic, and a gentle softness." I basked in her glow a while longer, letting the softness of her light fill me.

The early morning dawn crept into my sleeping bag as I drifted out of a dream of fields and fields of flowers. I lounged in my sleeping bag, waiting for the sun to warm the air and dry a bit of the dew. The events of the last two days floated through my head. What did all this mean? I felt I had been given many pieces to a puzzle that I now had to put together. I did my sun salutations and offered my morning prayers. Today was the day I was to return to camp, but I wasn't clear yet on what my vision really meant. How could I describe to anyone what had happened when nothing concrete was apparent to me? I lay in the bearberry patch one last time, waiting for the sun to reach directly overhead and make the moment when I was to begin my journey back to camp. Trying to make sense of all my experiences, I again felt as if something were just under the surface trying to emerge. Then I remembered my dream of fields of flowers and also recalled the extreme feeling of peace I had had after stopping to spend time with the clover while walking to my quest site. All the pieces began to slowly come together. This big change that we were moving into had to do with changing at the core of our being—DNA. It also had to do with living on a more peaceful planet. It seemed that the moon and flowers had a big part to play in this change, and I shouldn't be afraid to live this truth no matter how far-out it might seem. I saw that I needed to trust that as more of the vision emerges, all will become perfectly clear to me. After saying my final prayers, I thanked all my relatives for their partnership, packed up my gear, and headed back to camp, somewhat reluctantly. I was going to miss the peaceful serenity of this small piece of paradise.

Over the next few days, more and more fell into place for me, but it wasn't until I was sitting in the hot tub with Brooke that the vision became clear. She was talking to me about the moon and its effect on her, and we were also talking about flower essences and how they are so helpful during emotional times of change. In a flash, I saw what the vision quest was all about. I was to make a set of flower essences from moonlight instead of sunlight, and these essences would somehow affect DNA, which would cause change at a core level and move us along on our evolutionary path. In that moment the Moon Flower essences were birthed. Later, as I began to work with individual flowers, my understanding of our potential number of DNA strands and their alignment became clear. This is fully described in the following chapter.

For months after I left those rocks, I was still experiencing my vision. More and more pieces would bubble up as time went on and as I was able to integrate more of the experience. Each time I return to Blacktail, it feels like a homecoming. The deep communion that took place there with my relatives the rocks, the mountain, the moon, the hummingbird, and the bearberry fills me with a sense of family that goes way beyond blood. I also lovingly recall the deep bond that was forged among all the women who were questing. We shared in an experience of touching the divine in ourselves and Partner Earth. When we write to each other now, often we use our camp names—the names that were given to us after our vision quest, which represent our quest and the essence of our being. My name is Shares the Flower Song. The more I walk my Beauty Way, the more my name lives in me. I find that I am happiest and most at peace when I am sharing the flower song.

EQUAL PARTNERSHIP

One pitfall in working with the unseen realms is that we tend to think that what we can't see is better than we are. It's important to remember that we are working with the Devas in a co-creative partnership. When we carry the thought that they are better or wiser than we are, the relationship deteriorates into one of co-dependence. It's not that one is better than the other; it's just that we have different gifts to offer the partnership.

Humans are unique in that we have the ability to plan ahead. Our tendency is to expend thought energy on the future instead of being in the moment. This futuristic way of being is our inherent gift to evolving. We carry the gift of direction and purpose, propelled by a driving force of evolution. We are always looking to improve ourselves. Unfortunately, we have gotten lost in material gain as a way to get ahead.

We also have the unique trait of free will, which means that we always have a choice. We can choose whether or not we want to be in devic partnership, which is never imposed on us from the devic realm. Being in relationship with Lumelligence is as simple as asking.

The inherent gift of Devas is that of understanding the energetic pattern necessary to bring something into balanced form. This is the gift of design, or the "how-to" of manifestation. Perfect manifestation is created by combination of direction with an evolutionary force and design with balance. Each of these gifts is necessary to bring into being forms both physical and conceptual that do not destroy the Earth and all her beings. Creative force, not destructive force, is what perfect manifestation is all about.

When I'm working in my garden, if I try to "figure out" how to bring it into balanced form I find the process much less flowing. Sometimes I even experience resistance to getting the task done. However, when I provide the purpose and direction and the Devas provide the "how-to" for balanced manifestation, each of our inherent gifts is put to use. This is what Machaelle Small Wright refers to as "energy conservation at its best." It takes much more energy to try to "figure out" balanced manifestation than it does to ask the Devas.

Clare writes,

> I have always thought of working with the devic realm as an incredible expenditure of energy, and I have avoided doing it because of the way I was introduced to it. What this process [apprenticeship] has enabled me to understand is the co-creativity part. It means that there are partners to work with who have energies I do not, just as I have hands and trowels that they don't have. As your place shows me, when I commit some part of my attention to working with the beings of my place, they will co-commit and the work I do can move forward with some ease.

My spiral garden is where my work with the devic realm began. It's here that I find my greatest comfort and peace. My rhythm, now, is to enter the garden in an open communicative way. I know that the information I receive from the Lumelligence of my garden is their gift to me and that my embodiment and direction is my gift to the Devas. Together we move through our tasks with light-hearted ease, being grateful for the co-creative partnership we share.

JOYFUL ACTIVITY

Devas are well known for their lighthearted, joyful energy. In all my experience I've never felt any negative, judgmental, or heavy energy. The vibrations are always of love and harmony. This is my favorite part of partnering—it's fun! Folks have gotten the idea somehow that they have to work at devic partnership, and often it's this very attitude that blocks their experience. Lightening up about the whole process is the point. By being in partnership we are becoming enlightened. Carrying light energy is about love, joy, peace, and harmony.

Caralyn says, "I have experienced a sense of humor and joy from the Devas. I am often greeted, initially, from different voices, with how wonderful they think it is that I buried my daughter's placenta near a certain tree on our property. I feel like I get little pats on the back, for it is always at moments when I've completely forgotten about it for some time."

Several years ago, when I was first learning to ski, it was always such a struggle. I just couldn't understand why people would pay to slide down an ice- and snow-covered mountain with two thin little sticks on their feet. I, of course, would never have done this on my own, but my family was heavily into skiing, so it was ski or sit home. After a couple of years of battling to get down the mountain, I realized I had been going about it all wrong. I needed help with "how to" be with this mountain without such resistance. On one of those crystalline days when every speck of snow sparkles with inner lights and the trees wear overcoats of white, I found myself all alone and took a moment to drink in the beauty all around me. In that instant, I felt the Deva of the Mountain in all her majesty. The realization hit me like a lightening bolt. Why not ask the Deva of the Mountain to help me with skiing? I asked to be connected, and away I went. For the first time I felt what it was like to be one with the downhill. I skied as never before and was filled with such exhilaration and joy that on reaching the bottom of the mountain I was moved to tears of happiness. I realized it was not only my joy that I felt but also the mountain's joy. Together we had taken struggle and changed it into pleasure—all by my merely asking.

Devas are also very active. They want to engage with us because this is how manifestation actually happens. Usually, information we receive from Devas requires some type of action—physical, emotional, mental, or spiritual.

When you enter into partnership, prepare to take action of some sort.

While an apprentice at Green Terrestrial, Michele experienced the Deva of Burdock during an investigation into plant allies. Her encounter warranted action in the moment, which brought action later with the same work of the day and also brought action in her life in a positive way. She tells her story of Lappa (Latin for burdock) thus:

> What happened between me and Lappa on that sunny day at Green Terrestrial has rooted in me far more deeply than I had realized. The exchange not only multiplied my understanding of the world of weeds and intensified my relationship with burdock, it also profoundly affected my artist self, enhancing creative pathways which had before been only flickering ideas lurking in my subconscious. I use my friend and ally, burdock, as an aid to well-being, not only for my physical self but for my spiritual self as well. She provides a model for strength: rooted, strong, joyous, luxurious, available, medicinal, and mature. At the time of the exchange between us—when a personification of the Deva of Lappa Burdock developed on my paper—I realized a new dimension to intuitive art. Later, I said to you [Pam] that I could be an artist for herbalists. You responded, "Yes, and it is important that you know the plants." This new pathway has grown and carried me even further. I now work for herbalists, and others, devoting the work to the spirit of well-being. I am also now a partner in the creation of beautiful medicine shields for people who commission them, and have begun conducting intuitive and medicinal art workshops, weed walks, and talks and herbal classes. The pen name for my business, Wisesight, also evolved out of this experience. The experience at Green Terrestrial with burdock was a true turning point in my life, work, health, spirituality, and consciousness.

Michele's experience with the Deva of Burdock was not expressed in words but instead through a beautiful work of art, which later became the cover of one of my catalogs. Michele's action with burdock touched every aspect of her life. She saw a whole new way to express her artistic ability as well as to develop a viable business for herself. Her partnership with Burdock continues to reverberate throughout her life.

Illustration by Michelle Leavitt

OTHER EXPRESSIONS OF LUMELLIGENCE

In my search for understanding the essence of Devas, I come across
Angels again and again. These messengers of God were once relegated primarily to religious experience, usually of the Christian faith,
and told about only in the Bible. Now, Angels are everywhere. I
went into a bookstore recently and saw there an entire section for
Angels alone. On the shelves were eighty-seven different books on
Angels. *Time* writer Nancy Gibbs tells us,

> There are angels-only boutiques, angel newsletters, angel seminars,
> angels on *Sonia Alive*. A *Time* poll indicates that most Americans
> believe in angels. Harvard Divinity School has a course on angels;

Boston College has two. Bookstores have had to establish angel sections. In the most celebrated play on Broadway, Tony Kushner's Pulitzer-prize-winning *Angels in America*, a divine messenger ministers to a man with AIDS. In *Publishers Weekly*'s religious best-seller list, five of the ten paperback books are about angels. Even Hillary Rodham Clinton has a gold pin she wears on days she needs help: "angels' wings," she explains.

With the simultaneous rise in popularity of Angels and the ever-growing awareness of Devas, I have to ask how similar in nature these beings are. Dorothy Maclean, in her book *To Hear the Angels Sing*, uses the terms *angel* and *deva* interchangeably. My sense is that both Angels and Devas are intelligent beings of light who are a little different in their focus. Angels tend to deal directly with humans, whereas Devas are involved more with the realm of nature and conceptual thought. When I look at the diversity of humans and their specialties, I realize it is the same with Lumelligence. Devas are the architects, and Angels are the counselors. Likewise, when I work with elementals, also known as nature spirits, I am aware that their function is more directly related to physical structures, like how much water a plant needs for its optimum growth.

Another area of increasing popularity is shamanism. Although the roots of shamanism are in the indigenous cultures of Asia, traces of it are found in primary cultures worldwide. This is a belief system that actively engages with the spirit world for purposes of healing and transformation. Paul Devereux, in his book *Earthmind,* refers to shamans as spiritual ecologists. In an attempt to understand the nuances of spirit, an apprentice, Gary, wrote,

> I have also had experiences in connecting to plants that feel more shamanic than devic. It happened the first time in connecting to the motherwort plant and again with your wormwood. Recently, it happened again with a young juniper I was planting. While I'm connecting with the energy of the particular plant, these few times, it has gone beyond just that plant. It is a sense that I am feeling the energy or the message of the whole of that plant species. Like all junipers are connected to this one energy, or that they all have one soul. With the motherwort, it was like there was a song and a message that comes out of the Earth and that all motherworts pipe into

the environment. . . . When I took the class with you on devic work this time I felt more comfortable with it. I had always made a separation with this work and shamanic work with the plants. Sometimes I've felt that I could connect to the soul of the plant— something that felt like an expression out through the plant that came from deep in the earth. When I've had these experiences, I always felt that they were different, separate from what you were teaching with Devas and nature spirits. But when I took the class with you this time, it suddenly occurred to me that it was all part of the same thing. Spirit exists at all levels wherever you tune in. So that if you are tuning into the design and pattern level, you get the Devas, if you are tuning into the level of function and place, you get the nature spirits, and if you tune into individual essence level, you get what I was getting, which feels more shamanic in nature; it's just another point on the continuum.

DEVAS IN EVERYDAY LIFE

There is a misconception that Devas are confined to the realm of gardening or nature. But since Devas hold the energetic design for physical and conceptual thought form, there is a Deva of anything that's in physical form or thought form. There are Devas of Home, Work, Health, Education, Communication, and so on. You can be in a co-creative partnership with them in every aspect of your life.

Amy's family owns a large commercial fruit farm in the Hudson Valley, and at one time she was the manager. The influx of mice into the orchard was at such a high level that if she didn't do something about it there would be considerable damage to the trees. Ultimately, this would translate into economic loss. Her choices were to have an airplane fly overhead and broadcast poisoned corn or to bait specific sites with poison. Being an advocate of ecological growing, she struggled deeply with what appeared to be a no-win situation. If she broadcasted poison, the song birds, as well as the mice, would eat the corn and die. With baiting or broadcasting, the poison-filled mice could be eaten by other animals, thus causing more damage to the surrounding wildlife population. She was torn with confusion. Any other farmer wouldn't have spent more than a few minutes deciding which method of death to choose. Knowing that she needed help, she dropped to Partner Earth and prayed to be shown the best option. In that moment, she let go of her control, gave herself in trust to Lumelligence, and stopped trying to figure out what to do. As she opened her eyes from her prayer, she heard the shrill cry of a hawk. She looked overhead, and there were three hawks circling above her. They circled and circled just over her head, not moving from where she was. She focused intently upon them and then knew the answer to her prayer. She would do nothing and let the hawks take care of the mice. She knew that this choice would probably mean loss of trees, but the answer was so loud and clear that she couldn't dismiss it. Over the next year and a half, almost a thousand trees were completely girdled by mice, so that on the surface, one might have said that her trust in Lumelligence was ridiculous. However, the trees that died were all of the Tydeman variety. None of the new trees or productive varieties were touched. Then the market for Tydeman apples completely dried up. They had become obsolete and unsaleable. The Tydeman orchard would have cost the farm money instead of making money—except that the mice killed the trees. In the moment of her prayer, Amy could never have anticipated the full outcome of her trusting because she didn't have the overall design for balanced manifestation. As it turned out, the song birds thrived and helped keep the orchard in balance by preying on insects that damage trees, the mice ate well all winter, the hawks ate well all spring, bringing back the natural balance of mice, the farm didn't lose money maintaining trees that produced unsaleable fruit, there was an abundance of firewood for the next winter, and Amy was at peace in her soul. What she did was a radical, revolutionary move. She dared to go against her formal training, she dared to listen to the inherent intelligent light force, she dared to let go of control and trust in the greater design, she dared to step into the evolutionary spiral and be in true partnership.

In my own work as a herbalist, I am constantly in partnership. When harvesting herbs from the wild, I can do my work much more efficiently when I'm connected to Lumelligence. A few years ago I needed a large supply of St. John's wort for a massage therapist who wanted oil to use in her practice. I went to my regular spots but found only small amounts. Not wishing to deplete the community, I didn't take any from those areas. Realizing I would need help, I asked to be connected to the St. John's wort Deva. Driving down Route 9W, a main road through the Hudson Valley, I went past a small group of shops next to a large field. At the far side of the field was a large outcropping of rocks. I felt a tug as I drove by but ignored it and drove on to the next spot where I hoped to find the herb I needed. Again, there was not enough to harvest. Back up Route 9W I went, and again there was that tug when I drove past the shops. Why not check it out, even though it didn't seem a likely spot? I parked my car in the lot and headed out across the field to the far side. When I got to the outcrop of rocks, I looked all over. There were a couple St. John's wort plants here and there, but again, not enough for my purposes. Why had I been led here to find only a few plants? I turned to leave, then felt an urge to look a little further and climbed the rocks to see what lay behind them. As I reached the top I could hardly believe my eyes. There stretched out in front of me was a small glade full of St. John's wort—more than enough for the oil I needed and all the tincture I needed to make as well. I thanked the St. John's wort Deva and harvested with love and gratitude in my heart.

Often people ask me what makes my preparations so much different from others. They say they can feel the difference even from extracts that are from "state of the art" labs. You can use razor-sharp steel choppers to masticate the herb; the exact ratio of alcohol to water to extract the precise amount of active ingredients; a thousand-gallon tumbler that constantly churns, extracting medicinal properties quickly and efficiently; a hundred-ton press to squeeze every drop of extract from the herb; and a bottling and labeling machine to effortlessly fill the bottles and label them. The whole process has been done with the highest-tech equipment and in the most efficient way possible, but one thing is missing. Not one person has touched the herbs. Without the ingredient of love, these preparations are merely a combination of chemical constituents in a bottle. When I work with herbs, I'm in partnership with the plant, the environment, and the Deva of healing. As I harvest herbs, I harvest them with love, healing intent, and gratitude. Once in the lab, I observe them as they are tincturing and then personally handle them three more times before they go out into the world. Each time they are treated lovingly, as any partner would be. They are infused with the recognition that the healing they create is not just for one person but is, indeed, everyone's healing.

The more I work with plants, the more I see the potential for profound partnership to take place. The herbal movement is wonderful, and it is helping to change the direction of health care in America. However, in our zeal to bring herbs to the mainstream, many of our natural habitats of wild herbs are being drastically depleted. We must take action right now to avoid contributing to what we condemn—overharvesting and elimination of species.

My current experiment is with the difference in medicinal quality between cultivated herbs and wild-harvested herbs. It has already been established with vegetable plants that when two plants that are grown in the same soil with the same additives of nutrients and water, but with one completely ignored except for bare maintenance and the other treated with loving care and companionship as a friend, the one lovingly cared for has more vitamins, minerals, and nourishing qualities than the ignored plant. One of the reasons for overharvesting is a belief that herbs from the wild have more potent medicinal qualities than their cultivated counterparts. I maintain that given the proper soil conditions and water requirements, along with loving partnership and strong healing intent infused into these plants as they are growing, they will have just as much medicinal quality, if not more. Producing medicinal herbs in this way takes the pressure off the natural habitats, allows for an active partnership to take place between the grower and the plants, and brings herbs with the highest possible medicinal quality to others.

Ian tells me of her profound experiences with the devic realm in forming her herbal product business. She and a friend decided to be partners in business, but at first she was reluctant. She had not had positive experiences with partners in business, but she was willing to try when Elizabeth told her she wanted to work with the Devas. They created a team of Devas that was specific to what they thought were essential ingredients for their business. This team, among others, included the Devas of Success, Money, Spirituality, Partnership, and Plants. They called it the Crowhorse team, this being the name of their company. They did a ritual and called in the Crowhorse team. Immediately there was a presence in their circle, which was undeniably the energetic aspect of Crowhorse, and in that moment they knew their business was born. They proceeded to work with the Crowhorse team on every aspect of creating the business, from the logo design to the choice of products, which products to make themselves, which to buy from others, what ingredients to use, and how to distribute their products. They also designed their workspace with their devic team, which helped them with the placement of workbenches and materials, the choice of plants, and even the choice of crystals to be in the space. They completely committed themselves to working co-creatively. Their first major selling experience was at the Women's Herbal Conference. They began preparing for the event two weeks ahead, but when consulted, the Crowhorse team instructed them to produce about four times as much as was humanly possible in the time available. They worked night and day, trusting implicitly in their co-creative process. Ian and Elizabeth were able to make about half of the amount they were told to make. They asked the Devas whether they were going to sell all these products at the conference, and the answer was no. Again, they trusted that in the larger design there was a reason to make so many products ahead of time. They came home from the conference with half of what they had made. Shortly thereafter, both their personal lives began to disintegrate to such a point that neither was able to put much energy into the business. They also lost their workspace, so they couldn't make their products even if they had wanted to. It now became apparent why the Crowhorse team wanted them to make so many products when they had the opportunity. Now they had enough to fill their orders and to take to the next conference. Ian continues to work with the Devas and feels that they are "an integral part of who I am and how I function on a daily basis."

In the arena of health, Lumelligence is always helpful in understanding what course of action to take. When I am doing consultations with people, I always ask to be connected to the Deva of Health. I also connect with my own Deva and the Deva of the person, assuming I have her or his permission. With willing clients, we connect together. It adds more power to the experience—it's like turning the volume up on the radio. I listen carefully to what the client tells me, and I also listen carefully to what vibrational resonance is coming through Lumelligence. Often, as a person is speaking, different herbs will march in front of my inner vision. I take note of them and, along with my empirical knowledge and my understanding of traditional uses of the herbs, make suggestions that will be helpful in this situation.

When I have bodywork done, I have my practitioner connect with the Deva of Healing and my devic aspect in order to pinpoint what exactly is needed for me on that particular day. The results are far more effective than those from just a routine massage.

In any situation, you can call on the Deva of Health to assist in showing you how to bring balance back to your being. Even when you are dealing with doctors who may not believe in Lumelligence, you can ask to be connected to the Deva of Health. Through that connection, you will have a sense of knowing whether the doctor's recommendations for you will bring the most balance in your healing process.

Devas can be called upon in any situation at any time. I was surprised while doing a workshop in Brooklyn to receive this strong communication from the Deva of the City:

> You need to be in relationship to everything, including those things you think you don't like. It's even more important to be in partnership with me in order to bring the city back to balance instead of leaving me to fall into decay. Don't be afraid to come here and do your work. You felt the difference driving in today. You know you can be in good relation and not have fear. Look at me with eyes of love, and I will mirror the same to you. There are many aspects of me that are very alive, and there are many people ripe for my aliveness. Tell people about me, too, not just the Broccoli Deva. You don't have to always be here to be in relationship with me. But be a friend to me and call me up once in a while. I have much to share with you. There are many people here eager to work with me, but they don't know how to. Perhaps you could assist them in that process.

This very direct message made me realize how important it is for me to be open to *all* devic presence because it is, indeed, everywhere and in everything. Another time in the city, my friend Hollis and I were having dinner together and needed to park on the street. I was moaning about not being able to find a spot and she said, "Oh, that's easy—just ask the Deva of Parking." I chuckled and said, "OK, I'll give it a try." We turned the corner, and a car pulled out directly in front of the building we were going to enter. Some would call that just coincidence, but according to the dictionary, coincidence involves two events occupying the same space and time. Essentially, this is being on the same wavelength, or matching resonance. The misunderstanding about coincidence is that it is not random but instead Lumelligence's movement away from chaos into order. We make the evolutionary step when we take the order of coincidence and move it into balanced partnership by conscious communication.

When we open to the devic realm, the key ingredient is the love vibration. Gary Zukav, in his book *Seat of the Soul,* reminds us that "divine intelligence is found in the heart, not the mind." Our love for Partner Earth and all our relatives will bring us back to balance and wholeness. Lorna Green, in her book *Earth Age,* says that we "have to get in touch with how much we love the Earth if we are to make our necessary changes." She points out that if we look at the five-billion-year existence of the Earth as if it were a twenty-four-hour period of time, humans have been here for eleven seconds. The last century represents a split second. From this vantage point, within a split second the Earth has been pushed to the brink of disaster by the species of free will and choice. Will we choose to remain a sentient species, or will we become extinct like so many of our brothers and sisters? I exercise my gift of free will and choice by this affirmation: "I choose life; I choose love; I choose balance; I choose spirit; I choose to come home to my true family and partner, the Earth."

5

THE AGE OF FLOWERING

This new age that we are moving into has been referred to by Dhyani Ywahoo as the Age of Flowering. Dhyani is the clanmother of the Etowah band of Cherokee. Her lineage has been unbroken for twenty-seven generations, and she carries this ancient knowledge forward. When she refers to this age as a flowering one, she means not only that it is a time of awakening for all beings but also that the flowers will aid us in this process. The flowers are here as spokes-beings for all our relatives. They carry a vibration that is particularly easy for humans to communicate with, and they can translate what other relatives have to say. Their frequency is only slightly different from ours, making the connection between us fairly accessible.

Flowers can be used in many ways, but the easiest and most widely used form is flower essences. Flower essences are prepared by placing flowers in water with sun, moon, or starlight shining on them so that their energetic essences are infused into the water. Traditionally, they have been made with sunlight and taken by humans and animals. This form of vibrational healing is highly effective on the more subtle bodies of the emotional, mental, and spiritual aspects of our whole being. An imbalance begins on one of these levels and manifests physically only when it has gone unattended for quite sometime. Each flower carries a unique signature, vibration, or gift to help in the shifting of a specific energy pattern. Flower essences help to integrate, stabilize, and balance energy. They can assist us in changing the imbalanced energy created by deep emotional trauma, negative thought patterns, and spiritual separation. They also can aid in the physical healing process by shifting obstructions in the electrical and central nervous system of our bodies. The best-known flower essences are the Bach Flower Remedies, developed by Dr. Edward Bach in the 1930s. His essences primarily address emotional and psychological difficulties. As we continue to evolve, our areas of growth and our need for balancing shift and change. For many, the emotional and mental issues have been cleared to such a degree that they can now address the areas of soul development and spiritual awareness. With this evolutionary impulse, many new flower essences are being developed specifically for this purpose.

MOON FLOWER ESSENCES

I was on vision quest in the Montana Rockies when I first received the inspiration to create the Moon Flower Essences. I saw clearly how out of balance the planet is and that the energy that the moon carries is needed for rebalancing. The light of the moon has a subtle, nonaggressive energy. Its signature is that of feminine deep knowing that allows the dormant wisdom to be gently stimulated and integrated in a way that doesn't create an upheaval one is not ready for. The moon also vibrates with intuition, magic, and dreamtime. It opens us to primal knowing by magnetizing spirit and form. Partnering with the moon brings a soft blending that whispers spirit wisdom. When flower essences are made with moonlight, all of the qualities of the moon are part of the essence as well as the qualities of the individual flowers.

The making of the Moon Flower Essences was a co-creative effort with the moon; the Deva of each flower; Sirius, who fuels the fire in my soul and is directly involved with evolution on this planet; and Lela, my wise woman within. Each of these elements as well as my own primal knowing had a part in the manifestation of these flower essences. By partnering with all of these relatives I stood in the place of oneness where there is no separation from my

INNER TRADITIONS INTERNATIONAL

DESTINY
B O O K S

DESTINY
RECORDINGS

DESTINY
AUDIO EDITIONS

Park Street Press

En Español

If you wish to receive a copy of the latest INNER TRADITIONS INTERNATIONAL catalog and to be placed on our mailing list, please send us this card. It is important to print your name and address clearly.

Date _____

Name _____

Address _____

City _____ State _____ Zip _____

Country _____ Email address _____

Inner Traditions International, Ltd.
P.O. Box 388
Rochester, VT 05767
U.S.A.

knowing and theirs. Together we brought forth these essences to aid in the massive evolutionary leap we are now involved in.

To fully understand the Moon Flower Essences, one must realize that the evolutionary spiral is directly linked to the realignment of fragmented strands of DNA. These essences are specifically for the purpose of aiding in the re-membering of the filaments of light, of the DNA, that have been split asunder. We hold the capacity for twelve complete strands of DNA, the thirteenth being the unification of the twelve—our link to the creator. Each strand is a filament of light that carries a specific frequency of sound and light. Each filament corresponds to a chakra or energy center in our being—our whole being, not just our physical body. Each strand also is associated with one of the systems of our whole being. Each filament has an affinity for partnering with a particular relative, and there are specific energetic qualities associated with each strand. I sense that more and more we will begin to realize the many aspects that each strand holds and is in common union with. In this ever-expanding dynamic process of evolution, old forms are rapidly changing and new ones are constantly emerging. Table 1 shows all of the Moon Flower Essences and the strands they help realign.

Let's take one of the flower essences and see how we might best work with it. The essence Lavender carries the sound frequency of "ah-h-h," and the color frequency of green. The chakra it is connected to is the heart. Its association in the body is with the circulatory system. Its partnering aspect is the Earth, and the quality it has affinity with is joy in dailiness. There is a DNA strand that holds the ancestral memory of all of these pieces to integrate into the whole in a balanced and harmonious way. If you feel that you don't experience joy in your daily life, you could take Lavender essence. You could enhance the process by wearing green or visualizing yourself surrounded by green. You could also tone the sound "ah-h-h," holding your heart. Breathe into your heart chakra and visualize it embraced by green loving light. Feel the blood moving through your veins and pumping through your heart as you align your circulatory system with the filament of light that holds the memory of its balanced functioning. Allow yourself to partner with the Earth by asking to be

Table I

Sound	Color	Chakra	Flower essence	Whole being association	Partnering aspect	Quality
o-o-o	Red	Root	Tithonia torch	Skeletal muscular	Humanmade inanimate form	Grounding
oh-h-h	Orange	Hara	Sunflower	Reproductive system	Natural inanimate form	Releasing old patterns
aw-w-w	Yellow	Solar plexus	Borage	Digestive system	Water	Trust
ah-h-h	Green	Heart	Lavender	Circulatory system	Earth	Joy in dailiness
ih-h-h	Blue	Throat	Heart's ease	Respiratory system	Air	Compassion
eh-h-h	Indigo	Third eye	Calendula	Immune system	Fire/Sun	Self-love
e-e-e	Purple	Crown	Loosestrife	Nervous system	Moon	Attention to synchronicity
Drum	Pink	Astral	Hyssop	Emotional stability	Mineral	Giving and receiving energy
Windpipe	Light yellow	Ethereal	Morning glory	Mental clarity	Plant tree	Staying in evolutionary energy flow
Rattle	Light green	Transcendent	Cosmos	Spiritual awareness	Animal	Receiving guidance
Bells	Sky blue	Planetary	Purple coneflower	Earth essence	Human	Touching into source energy
Crystal resonance	Lavender	Universal	Foxglove	Soul path	Conceptual thought form	Partnering with all life
om-m-m	White	Creator	Butterfly bush	Cosmic consciousness	Cosmos	Balancing and harmonizing energy

linked in partnership. Then ask how you can be a better partner, or ask what the earth needs to be in a balanced place, knowing that your act is one more step in the realignment of DNA that remembers when the Earth and you weren't separate. To take this from a different perspective, perhaps you don't even realize that you're missing joy in your dailiness, but you are experiencing heart palpitations, and the lack of circulation in your body is causing numbness in your fingertips. This could be your body's way of telling you that you've become too distant from the Earth. Once you begin using the essence, you realize how weak your connection to the Earth has been, and you begin to take walks and lie on the Earth to listen to her guidance.

Another way to work with the essences is to specifically partner with one of your relations you don't feel in touch with, or one that you feel has been so abused that you want to heal that split—for example, the mineral Coal. Taking Hyssop flower essence can help you be in communication with Coal because the DNA strand that Hyssop helps align is connected to the mineral kingdom. You can either work with the essences on a whole-strand level or just work with one aspect of the DNA strand that you know needs aligning or balancing.

You can use the essences to emphasize the qualities that the Moon offers by taking the essence that corresponds with the lunation you are in. A lunation is one complete cycle of the moon—approximately twenty-eight days. The flowers go through different stages throughout the year. The titles I've given them represent the energy field they're in during that lunation. For example, in spring you might want to take Cosmos flower essence during the "Flowers Pop Out Their Heads Lunation" or, in the fall, Sunflower during the "Flowers Drop Their Seed Lunation." This is an acknowledgment of where the flowers are in their seasonal cycle and how you can partner within that cycle yourself. During the winter months in the "Flowers Begin Dreaming Lunation," take Heart's Ease essence, be less active, and perhaps keep a dream journal. The thirteen lunations and their corresponding flower essences are listed in Table 2.

By working to realign your DNA, you consciously acknowledge your desire to evolve and become a fully enlightened being. You reclaim your birthright to live in balance and harmony with all your

Table 2 THE THIRTEEN LUNATIONS

Lunation	Moon Flower Essence
Flowers Lie Sleeping lunation	Calendula
Flower's Juice Thaws lunation	Morning glory
Flowers Stretch Their Limbs lunation	Lavender
Flowers Begin to Move lunation	Borage
Flowers Pop Out Their Heads lunation	Cosmos
Flowers Reach For the Sun lunation	Hyssop
Flowers Spread Their Petals lunation	Butterfly bush
Flowers Share Their Nectar lunation	Purple coneflower
Flowers Make Their Seed lunation	Tithonia torch
Flowers Drop Their Seed lunation	Sunflower
Flowers Return to the Earth lunation	Foxglove
Flowers Close Their Eyes lunation	Loosestrife
Flowers Begin Dreaming lunation	Heart's ease

Each Moon Flower Essence corresponds to one of the thirteen lunations (cycles of the moon). You may choose to work with the essences according to the lunation you are in.

relatives. You place yourself as an integral part of the whole that would not be the same whole without you. You take your rightful place as a co-creator of this universe, where all of life is recognized as divine.

I have purposely kept the descriptions brief for each of the Moon Flower Essences to encourage others to use their intuition and expand on the uses of the essences. Because of the evolutionary quality in applying these essences, there is always room for growth. The following stories are examples of how the Moon Flower Essences can affect one's life.

⚘

Cyndie, a flower essence practitioner, uses the Moon Flower Essences with clients. She has observed their ways of working on unique situations within an overall pattern. She says of the essences,

"They seem to center around the unknown, issues of avoidance, denial and the shadow side, bringing light and awareness to the individual's issues. They seem to go into the corners and shed light on what's really going on in that corner."

✦

My friend Kate was making a major change in her life. She was planning a move with her family to an unfamiliar area to begin a community with relatively new friends. Her husband was very enthusiastic about the move, but she was reluctant to leave her old friends, home, and community that she had put so much love and energy into. As they were in the midst of formalizing plans for selling their house and moving, her back went out. She had to spend several days in bed and then be extremely careful when she was up and about. This went on for several weeks until she knew that something had to give. She decided to take flower essences. She put together a combination that included Foxglove Moon Flower Essence.

Over a period of two days, Kate had profound understandings about her life: past, present, and future. She remembered how as a child her family often moved and that this experience was traumatic to her creative self. One day, as a child, she had come home and found her piano chopped up in the backyard because it wouldn't fit in the new house they were moving into. On another occasion she had to give up her dance lessons when her family moved. She saw clearly that moving had torn away the foundation of her being. She became keenly aware of the rich abundance of her life and how she had been gifted with knowledge and a wealth of experience that was incredibly valuable to herself, family, and community. She shared this wisdom unreservedly and with deep caring. Kate also saw that to hold onto this abundance in fear that it might go away was not necessary. It was a part of her being, no matter where she was. In a flash of insight she saw her soul's journey and how all that had come before was a preparation for this next phase of her life. Her commitment to her partner and to their path together in a self-sufficient community, whose intention was to embrace the full circle of life and reweave the tattered web into a sustainable way of living that recognizes and honors the Earth and all her beings, became grounded in the core of her being. She knew that this was the right move and that it would lead her to her true home. She no longer felt that the foundation of her being was crumbling; instead, she felt the foundation reinforced with solid blocks. As she made this shift her back was completely healed.

The flower essence Foxglove is associated with the DNA strand that helps you remember your soul's path. It is connected to your universal chakra so that energetically you remember your expanded being, which encompasses you on a universal level. It also has the quality of helping you to partner with all of life. In Kate's case, her universal energy center was expanding her awareness to see clearly her soul's path and that part of that path had to do with partnering with all of life. This was her unique experience with Foxglove and its expression through her to realign her DNA. Kate has often used the Moon Flower Essences with other people and finds that they help them to merge the deeper dreamtime aspect of themselves with their conscious awareness.

*

Marsha had been taking the Bach Flower Remedies but decided to switch to the Moon Flower Essences when a friend gave them to her as a gift. Almost immediately, a subtle shift began to take place. The first day she noticed a whole body lightness. The next day she noticed how she continually smiled at herself. By the third day she realized that her normally academic serious self felt really good. She attributed this change in her expression of self to the Moon Flower Essences. Those early days of taking the essences were laying the foundation for what was to come. She was taking all of the essences except Hyssop most of the time, and they were realigning the filaments of light in Marsha's cells to prepare her for a very important piece of work.

Marsha is a whale and dolphin researcher with the Ocean Mammal Institute and she has a deep understanding of these amazing beings. However, she felt that a major shift was needed to bring her to a deeper relationship with them. She began to partner with the dolphins in a new way. While in Maui she had a vision while looking out at the ocean. The ocean ceased its movement, and she saw the form of a dolphin made by the sea foam. Around the dolphin was a purple net. She knew the dolphins were helping her to create a network of people to continue her work with the whales and dolphins. In a series of synchronistic events that followed, three women were led to her who each played an integral role in furthering the endeavors of the Ocean Mammal Institute. All three of these women, at different times, had swum with the same pod of dolphins off Baja, California. This series of events has led Marsha to realize that her work with the dolphins is taking on a new form. She is being called by them to be a bridge between worlds. She needs to lighten her frequency in order to understand their communication, and the Moon Flower Essences are helping her to do this.

ᴥ

Lynnwa says about Sunflower Moon Essence, "I had been working on issues with old patterns trying to change into new pathways. This Moon Essence was a magic wand that accelerated the breakage of personal patterns, old negative repeats, that no longer promoted my growth."

ᴥ

Peggy usually uses all the essences together, instead of only one or two at a time. She feels "an opening in consciousness for a new level of energy alignment with divine forces. The essences magnetize parts that are ready for integration and light is felt moving into its new space which was waiting for it." Peggy says she feels that "there are possibilities of alignment with a yet unformed reality." She feels that the essences facilitate the merging of the vibration of who she is with the potentials of the new realities being formed. When they are combined with the Perelandra Soul Ray Essences, she feels she is connecting to universal consciousness, which she experiences in a multidimensional way. While traveling between dimensions she feels grounded in the "realness" of her experience. For Peggy, the essences are an integral part of her life that she accepts as her allies on a daily basis. She is keenly aware of their profound effect on her life. She experiences the cellular shift both physically in her body and in her expanded multidimensional self. She feels the realignment of her DNA and the lightness that that brings. Peggy also senses the strands of DNA that are yet to be encoded and anticipates this unknown reality with excitement. She is consciously partnering with the flowers through the essences to aid in the process of becoming a fully co-creative human. She is reclaiming her birthright and returning home to the light.

❧

Jerielle notices that each time she uses the Moon Flower Essences she has a significant dream that helps her to deepen and understand another level of her being. In this instance, the dreamtime quality of the moon is working through the essences.

❧

Flower essences can be used not only with humans but with other relatives, too. They can be given to land, water, rocks, animals, and plants as well as your car, home, and office. Flower essences are here to integrate and stabilize transformative energy. They work on anything that has a vibratory aspect, thus encompassing all of life. I have been particularly attracted to using the Moon Flower Essences with abused relatives in whom the wound of separation needs to be healed and where the short-sighted will of humans has caused damage.

❧

I was deeply honored to have Sunflower essence travel to Auschwitz in Poland. A group of people were gathering there to heal the wounds of war. The original group consisted of children of the survivors from the concentration camp and children of Nazis who worked the camps. This in itself carried powerful healing energy. Their intention was to begin at Auschwitz and walk across Europe and Asia to the sea and then go by boat to Hiroshima, where they would gather with children of survivors of the atomic bomb. A flower essence combination was taken to the Auschwitz gathering by Sarah and Robbie, who were videotaping the event. Once they arrived, it was clear that the flower essence was not only for the people there but also for the land and the water. The water where the ashes from the incinerators were dumped was particularly in need of healing. The essence was given to the pond near Birkenau with love and healing intent. This simple yet profound act brought focused healing energy to the water that for so many years had carried the energy of human relatives caught in the atrocity of war. Sarah was also guided to offer the flower essences to the ruins of the gas chambers and the selection ramp where the trainloads of Jews arrived. Throughout the four-day event, Sarah experienced moments of terror rising up from within. Being of Polish Jewish descent, she was remembering through her ancestral line the trauma of Auschwitz. When she took the flower essence combination, she felt a soothing internal effect that helped calm the terror and begin healing the split in her being. The Sunflower essence is for releasing old patterns. It is clear to me that Sunflower was one of the essences in the combination that went to Auschwitz because the old pattern of warring with others must shift in order for this planet and all its beings to evolve. I realized that this experience was a homecoming healing. It was a gathering of people with the intent of healing a split among themselves. Once they were gathered, they saw the need to heal the split, not only among themselves but with their relatives, the land and water, as well. This type of experience has been in my visions. These gatherings of people coming together for the express purpose of returning home and healing the split with all their relatives are known as homecoming healings.

FLOWERS' MANY GIFTS

When I work and play with flowers I recall the words of George Washington Carver, who so dearly loved them: "When I touch that flower I am touching infinity. It existed long before there were human beings on this earth and will continue to exist for millions of years to come. Through the flower I talk to the Infinite, which is only a silent force. This is not a physical contact. It is not in the earthquake, wind, or fire. It is in the invisible world. It is that still small voice that calls up the fairies." Flowers have been inspiring humans since the beginning of time with their incredible beauty, sweet nectar, and potent fragrance. It's no wonder that in this great time of need they rally again and make themselves completely available to us to help heal the fragmented web of life.

While I was in Montana working with Brooke Medicine Eagle and a group of her campers at one of her Eagle Song Camps, we spent a day with the flowers. We allowed ourselves as a group to be attracted to a particular flower. We then opened to the Deva of the flower and asked for guidance. Linda's experience follows:

Today our group was to seek a flower from which to make a flower essence. After exploring several possibilities, we wandered over to a large purple Thistle. As we spent time with it, communicating with the Thistle Deva, it became clear that we were all strongly called to it. Upon close examination, it was discovered to hold specks of blue pollen which, when brushed on our hands, was like sticky silver glitter. We were all amazed. It was as if the light of life shone out from it! Sparks of life transferred from Thistle to us! We then found a cluster of thistle in an open field (the tipi meadow). We circled around it, sat down, and each spoke in the silence of our spirit to the Deva, asking to establish communication and partnership, asking if it would be willing to become a flower essence and share its energy. We then meditated for a long time, each sending loving energy to the flower and receiving the same. As I focused on a particular flower that was facing me, it began to fade, then became transparent, then disappeared completely! I could clearly see the grasses and plants behind it, which moments earlier had been obstructed from my view. After several seconds, it materialized again. Then it faded and disappeared. Then it returned—again and again and again and again. Several times, when it returned and was clearly before my eyes, I shifted my position to peer around it, to see for certain what was actually growing in the field behind it. Sure enough, it was exactly as I had seen—without moving my head—when Thistle disappeared! Clearly, Thistle was moving into another dimension and inviting me to experience its reality. Eventually, Thistle faded away and stayed away. After a while I became worried and thought, "Sister, don't leave me," and she returned right away. But then she faded again. Each time she stayed away too long, I called to her and she materialized.

The timing of this lesson was incredible. Just this morning I had a conversation with Laura about the *Celestine Prophecy* in which I said the whole book was in line with my personal experiences except for the Ninth Insight. This Insight teaches that the more evolved one becomes, the higher one vibrates, until becoming invisible to the rest of the world, one can walk bodily into heaven. I thought the author had stretched credibility too much here, and I couldn't quite believe the truth of the Ninth Insight. Now, here, as soon as I announced I needed a lesson, Thistle demonstrated the Ninth Insight beyond any doubt! No sooner asked than answered! I thought that Thistle must be so highly evolved, vibrating so fast as to be perfectly united with Creator/The Universe. As advanced as she was, love and connection was her essence and her lesson, for she never abandoned me, but returned each time I called her to show that in reality she had never left me. She showed herself to be one with me and with the Creator, and invited me into her reality, which in turn is my reality, and the reality of every Being in the Circle of Life.

Linda's profound experience of the Thistle's ascension brought her to a deep understanding of the multidimensional reality that we live in. Linda knew that this particular blossom was ready to transform, so we gladly accepted the gift of this blossom into our flower essence. She was still there for all of us sharing her lessons, only now in the form of a flower essence.

In Provincetown, doing a workshop on co-creative partnership, I encountered uva ursi (or bearberry). It was a sunny spring day, and the flowers were just beginning to pop their heads out of the ground. We were making flower essences, and the group had divided up to choose the flowers they were most attracted to. I sat with uva ursi, observing her delicate bell-shaped flowers with their hint of pink. I asked to be connected to the Deva of Uva Ursi and let myself move into that vibrational resonance. I felt a deep stirring—something was trying to emerge. As the sun warmed me, I was transported back to Montana and the Medicine Rocks, where I sat in an uva ursi patch while questing. I remember how I had had a similar feeling of something deeply stirring, trying to burst forth. From that experience in Montana, the Moon Flower Essences had emerged.

We made our flower essences and shared our communications with the flowers we had chosen. Uva ursi made me feel as if something were just under the surface that wanted to come into consciousness. I took the essence for the next several days. Then one morning, while I was in meditation, the concept of PEEC arrived. PEEC is Partner Earth Education Center, an organization focused on educating people about our changing relationship to Partner Earth through co-creative partnership, sustainable living, and renewable energy. This organization will disseminate information on practical daily ways to live more sanely, bringing both inner and outer peace. PEEC will provide a forum for rekindling our love for Partner Earth through nature experiences—some in the wild, some in the garden, and others in the backyard. PEEC will offer opportunities to travel to abused relative sites and conduct homecoming healing ceremonies. We will dedicate ourselves to being nonexclusive. This opportunity to renew our intimate relationship with Partner Earth without prejudice toward race, religion, sex, or economic standing will bring equality to the deep ecology movement. We will solicit funds from sources that are able to provide the economic base to bring co-creative partnership to people otherwise unable to participate because of lack of funds. PEEC will become a working demonstration community of sane living. This is the vision, just under the surface, that wanted to emerge while I was sitting with uva ursi in Provincetown. Uva Ursi essence helped this emergence to take place.

Flowers can be worked with and played with in many ways. They don't have to be made into essences in order for us to receive their beneficial effects. Sitting in a garden, quietly allowing oneself to connect to the whole being of the flower and receive its vibrational patterning, is just as helpful as taking a flower essence. I love to lie in a field of wildflowers and feel the whole community of flowers around me, nourishing me and supporting me. My favorite thing to do is to visit flowers in the early morning, sit quietly with them, and sip the dew from their petals. This dew carries the vibration of that flower and also the early dawn energies. It is refreshing and vitalizing. What a great way to start the day!

Kate tells me that she was carrying a lot of fear of the unknown and all the "what ifs" when she moved to New York. She felt a tightness at her core. She tried meditating, taking herbal nervines, and even willing the fear to go away. She talked with her partner about it several times until she began to sound like a broken record. Nothing seemed to help her relax into the move they were making. It was time for her to harvest the emerging Aspen flowers to make a flower essence for her business, Woodland Essence. When she approached the tree, she asked to be in connection with the spirit of the tree. She began to work and felt the tree vibrating with her. She became quieter and quieter inside, and peace began to settle in her being. She gathered several branches to harvest the buds. She sat and picked the buds from the branches, all the while being present with the moment. Robins who had just come home from their southern winter vacation sat in the trees near her and sang a song of reassurance. "We're here, spring has come again and all is well." At that moment, sixty or seventy geese flew overhead, honking the announcement of their return. Another affirmation: life goes on, the cycle continues. In this timeless moment, Kate felt the Aspen weaving its essence all around her. She clearly saw that the more she held fear, the less she would be open to the path in front of her. Aspen was resonating with Kate and filling her with peace and the ability to let go of her fear. The Aspen flower essence is specifically used for fearlessness, beginnings, and breaking the ice. It's referred to as Mother Courage. By partnering with Aspen and opening to her frequency, Kate was able to receive her gifts. She did not need to take Aspen flower essence internally to resonate with her and receive the benefits of her vibration.

⁂

Deborah had a profound emotional healing while meditating with Heart's Ease prior to making a flower essence in class. She felt it open her heart chakra and bring the deep pain and sorrow of her inner child to the surface. Because the energy of the land and group was so safe, she knew that she could enter into the pain and move through it and release it. There was so much love that it hurt, making her aware that it should be this way everywhere. She felt the pain move into her throat chakra and knew that this was where it got stuck. This was the place where grief could be expressed, the place where her creative outlet was blocked. She let herself cry and release the grief and pain, and then the unconditional love of the cosmos began to flow. She let this life force flow through her, bringing her to an orgasmic love state. In this moment she saw all the pain and sorrow of the world with an eye of compassion, realizing that her pain was everyone's and that when she healed herself others' pain and sorrow would be lessened. Deborah felt Heart's Ease to be a master healer that helped her work with core issues of the heart expressed through the throat—the creative outlet—and helped her come to know compassion. This experience led her to moving beyond the thought "I'm not good enough" to making beautiful beaded crystal necklaces for everyone in the group. This experience arose merely when she sat with Heart's Ease, partnered with her, and

Illustration by Cara Montgomery

allowed her gifts to be felt. Deborah was able to heal a split within her being, bringing her closer to wholeness.

⚜

We may also receive the benefits of flowers through other means. Many, many flowers are edible and medicinal. Eating flowers adds a light touch to any meal. There's something joyful about sitting down to a salad filled with a multitude of flowers in an array of colors. I've never seen it fail to bring a smile to one's face. The list of edible flowers is long, but a few of the more common ones that most people know are nasturtiums, dandelions, violets, borage, calendula, red clover, rose, johnny-jump-ups (also known as heart's ease), lilac, squash blossoms, and honeysuckle. These can be added to salads or prepared in other ways.

Let's look at dandelion, the most widely known and common flower. The blossoms can be dipped in a batter of your choice (I like a tempura batter) and fried to make fritters. Make a syrup taking one ounce of dried blossoms, putting them in a quart jar, and pouring boiling water over top of them. Let them steep for two hours. Then pour the liquid in a pot and simmer it until the volume is reduced by half. Add four ounces of honey per eight ounces of dandelion brew. This makes a fairly sweet syrup but the honey helps to preserve it (I prefer to use less honey—only two ounces per eight ounces of dandelion brew). Keep it refrigerated. Put this delicious syrup on pancakes or anything you like.

Dandelion wine is one of the nicest ways to use this wonderfully healing plant as a tonic to the liver and digestive system. My dear friend, Adele Dawson, who has passed on, had a great recipe for dandelion wine, which requires lots of young children and a field of dandelions to accomplish. The recipe begins with eight gallons of dandelion flower heads. In a large crock pour four gallons of boiling water over the dandelion flowers, cover, and let sit twenty-four hours. Strain into a large canning pot and add five quartered oranges, two quartered lemons, and some crushed ginger root. Boil for thirty minutes, strain, add seven pounds of sugar, and pour back into the crock. When it has cooled to lukewarm, stir in two packages of dry yeast that have been dissolved in two tablespoons of water. Cover and wait until it stops "working" or bubbling, approximately ten to twelve days depending on the temperature. When it has finished working, siphon into gallon jugs, cork loosely, and try to wait a month before sampling. Now you can pour your wine into individual wine bottles to enjoy throughout the winter. The longer it sits the more it mellows, but by Thanksgiving it will go well with stuffing.

I make an oil from the blossoms by putting fresh blossoms in olive or almond oil and letting it sit for six weeks. Fill a jar full of blossoms and cover them with oil. Set the jar on a saucer, because the oil will ooze out the top at the lid for a week or two while the gases are being released from the blossoms. Stir it every day, and pour back into the jar what has oozed out. After six weeks, pour off the oil, and put the flowers in cheesecloth, and squeeze all the oil out of them.

Let the oil sit for about an hour so any water that may have been in the plant can separate out. The water will be on the bottom and the oil on the top. Pour off the oil and discard the water. The oil makes a wonderful massage oil with a special affinity for the belly.

As you can see, dandelion can be used in many ways. What's great about dandelion is that it is available everywhere—it even grows out of city sidewalks. It also has a particular affinity for us as a liver tonic, which is particularly needed in these polluted times. It's a tenacious survivor that makes all of itself available to us in great abundance.

Another way to play with flowers is to make flower nectar tea. Pick fresh blossoms, cover them with water in a jar with a lid, and let them sit in the sun for two to six hours. You can have a sweet floral nectar (lavender) tea, a spicy nectar (basil blossoms) tea, or a bitter tonic nectar (lilac) tea (refer to *Flowers in the Kitchen* by Susan Belsinger). You can also use flowers to lighten and beautify drinks by freezing them in ice cube trays. Then at any time you can pop them out and add them to your summertime drinks.

Honeys and vinegars can also be infused with the essence of flowers, especially the flowers of culinary herbs like thyme, oregano, and sage. Place the flowers in a jar and pour honey or vinegar over the blossoms. Let it sit for four to six weeks. Then serve the honey with biscuits or use the vinegar in salad dressings. I particularly like violets, which make an awesome purple vinegar. It needs to be used soon after it turns color, because the color fades with time.

Medicinal preparations are made with flowers by using water, alcohol, or oil as a medium to steep the flowers in. A typical flower tincture is made of yarrow blossoms. Fill a jar full of fresh yarrow blossoms, cover it with one hundred-proof vodka, and let it sit for six weeks. At the end of the six weeks, strain off the liquid and discard the flowers. The tincture or alcohol extract can be used medicinally to treat colds, flus, fevers, gastritis, indigestion, arthritis, or cystitis. Its astringent qualities can aid in internal bleeding and excessive menstrual bleeding. An oil can be made from the directions given earlier for oils and then used for any external wounds, hemorrhoids, and inflamed bites. You can make a water-based preparation, called an infusion, with dried yarrow by putting one ounce of dried flowers in a quart jar and pouring boiling water over them. Cover and let steep for two hours. The infusion can be used medicinally for any of the above ailments by drinking two to four cups a day or by applying the liquid to external wounds. You can make a poultice for external use by chewing on a fresh flower and applying it to the skin or by soaking dried flowers in warm water and then applying to the skin.

Flowers have been used cosmetically and for their pleasing scent for centuries. Floral waters of rose or lavender used as an after-bath splash or a refreshing body spray can be made in the same way the flower nectar tea was or by adding a couple of drops of essential oil of orange blossom to spring water. You can make a face steam by putting dried or fresh calendula and elder flowers (about four handfuls) in a large bowl and adding four quarts of boiling water. Let it steep ten to twenty minutes, covered. Place your face over the bowl, and cover your head and the bowl with a towel. Breathe deeply and allow yourself to let the vibrations of the flowers enter through the pores of your skin. Feel all those lines in your face relax, feel the tissue being toned, and sense the enlightening effect. Continue the steam until the water cools. Now look at yourself in the mirror and see the flowers shining through you.

After your facial steam you may moisturize your face with a flower lotion. The originator of this lovely cream recipe is Rosemary Gladstar. The basic recipe is one cup of distilled water (this can be a floral distilled water like rose, instead of plain), three-fourths cup oil, one third cup coconut oil, three-fourths ounce beeswax, one-fourth teaspoon vitamin E oil, one-eighth teaspoon essential oil. Moisturizing cream is made by combining oil and water together. Begin by melting over a very low flame the oil, coconut oil, and beeswax. The oil can be plain almond, apricot, or grapeseed or it can be a herbally infused oil like calendula or St. John's wort. After the beeswax has melted, cool it until you can stick your finger in it. At this point, add vitamin E and any essential oil you prefer for its scent and its healing quality. Lavender is nice. Begin by whirring the water in a blender. Slowly drip the oil mixture into the whirring water. At a certain point, it will homogenize and make a glubbing sound. Then, turn the blender off, scrape the sides, and then turn it on again and blend a little more. This makes a thick, very rich moisturizing cream. This recipe is basic and you can vary it as much as you like as long as you keep the same basic proportions of water to oil.

Essential oils, the oil of the plants, are used in aromatherapy and for their pleasing scent. They can be added to oils, waters, and baths to enhance the smell. It's important to realize that massive amounts of plant material are needed in order to make a small amount of essential oil. If you have access to the flowers themselves, it is most desirable to use the healing qualities of the flower aroma by smelling them while they are growing.

Surrounding yourself with flowers is a truly joyful experience. I believe that part of every building where people live and work should include flowers that they have access to. It's important to be able to smell them and touch them, not just view them from a distance. Bringing flowers into your home and workspace is important. Their gay colors and aroma add delight and sweetness to your life. During the flowering season I always have a bouquet of flowers on the kitchen table.

I had the good fortune to visit the Ware Collection of glass flowers at the Harvard University Botanical Museum. The glass models are a remarkably accurate botanical collection of 847 species of plants. The life-size models were blown or shaped after the glass was heated to create exact anatomical replications of enlarged sections of flowers and flower parts. The glass flowers were made by Leopold and Rudolph Blaschka of Germany for Professor George Lincoln Goodale, founder of the Botanical Museum, who wanted lifelike representations of the plant kingdom for teaching botany. This amazing display took me by surprise. I had never seen the insides of flowers before and became mesmerized by their beauty. I was particularly attracted to the cross-sections of the ovaries of flowers. Each was a unique and exquisite mandala of life. I felt myself spiral into these flower ovaries, feeling my own ovaries as beautiful flower mandalas with infinite possibilities for perfection in form. I felt the kundalini energy rise as one after another of these glass representations took my breath away. In that moment I was aware of myself partnering with all the ovaries of flowers and women and how we are at one in our beauty. My energy rose to an ecstatic state of divine bliss. I reveled in this bliss until it was time for our tour group to leave. This blessed experience has brought me to a deeper re-membering of the place of creation within women and flowers. What's really amazing is that all of this took place in a Harvard museum. Connection can happen anywhere—not only in a secluded glade full of flowers.

There is quite a resurgence of fairy images and lore as we enter the new millenium. People are having more and more experiences with nature spirits as they seek a deeper understanding of their relationship to the natural world. Nature spirits are playful, fun-loving beings who understand the energetic patterning for physical form manifestation and are often found in gardens and undisturbed nature settings. They are particularly attracted to flowers of any kind and tend to them with joyful dedication. I have sensed nature spirits through movement and flickers of light but have never actually seen them, as they usually reveal themselves in the image of fairies. My daughter, on the other hand, had many encounters with them when she was younger.

One day we were driving in our four-wheel-drive Trooper across the stream to the nettle patch to do some harvesting. I came near a wet area with a small island in the middle of it and was about to run over the small island. Cara shouted, "Watch out, Mom! The little people." I was startled and said, "Where? What little people?" She said, "Right there on the island. Don't you see them? This is where the little people live." I looked and looked, but to my dismay I could not see what she saw. I apologized for my insensitive barreling along and assured the little people that I would be more careful next time. I observed the area Cara had indicated and noticed a different quality in the aliveness of this spot compared with the area around it. A certain light vibration emanated from the island. I realized that by paying close attention I could recognize areas where nature spirits liked to be.

There is also a feeling sense in areas where fairies abound. A past apprentice, Jane, says about my spiral herb and flower garden, "It seemed that inside this spiral and for ten to fifteen feet surrounding it there was an intense feeling of harmony. Any farther out than that felt more normal, like any other piece of organically respected land. The harmony I speak of seemed co-creative in that the plants seemed vibrant and healthy. I've never seen healthier roses." Jane's sense of harmony was brought about by the nature spirits' constant attention to a balanced manifestation process and by my participation in this endeavor in a partnering way. Together we were tending the flowers and herbs, bringing joy to ourselves and all who experienced the garden. My garden has become my haven. When I'm in it, all is well with the world and a deep peace pervades. I experience it as a place for nourishment and guidance as well as for joyful, playful partnering. Each flower offers its gift of beauty, love, and en-lightening vibration for the stabilized integration of positive change that moves us on the evolutionary spiral, bringing us closer to being fully co-creative humans who partner with all of life.

6

THE DEVIC ESSENCE OF ANIMALS

ANIMAL SENSITIVITIES

Animals are the closest relative to us in consciousness, and yet, beyond dogs, cats, and horses, we have grown to fear or, at best, sport with most animals. Respect for animals' domains, their part in the cycle of life, and their right to life has completely eroded from modern society. Because of this, undomesticated animals have grown to mistrust humans. Our work to bring back a sense of trust evolving into partnership will require unconditional love and patience.

One of the leading animal trainers in this country is Linda Tellington-Jones. Her ground-breaking work in training horses is revolutionizing the way humans relate to animals. She not only tunes into the vibrational essence of the animal but actually works at that cellular level where we all reside in the oneness. The key to her deep level of communicating and working with animals stems from this understanding, "The cells that form each living being all share the same universal 'intelligence.' Every cell 'knows' how to be a perfect part of a feather, a twig, a hand, or a paw. It knows its function in the individual body at the same time as it knows its function in the universe." This "intelligence" that Linda speaks of is the same as that of Lumelligence.

Cara's dog, Choiya, is one of the most sensitive dogs I've ever known. She is keenly aware of energies of all types. I can read certain devic presences by watching Choiya. When the nature spirits are in a particularly playful mood, Choiya will run in circles at top speed or run and jump to great heights. While I work in the garden, she lies nearby, offering her calm reassurance. During class time, she makes her rounds to each person in the circle, letting them know she is there to help center their hearts. While we are out on walks, her alertness helps me to focus on the many unseen elements surrounding us. On one occasion, Choiya was with Edie, an apprentice, walking in the woods. Choiya suddenly stopped and began to whine, looking intently into the underbrush. Edie stopped and stared in amazement. There in the bush was a small figure, one of the many elementals that abounds in these woods. Choiya did not run after the nature spirit but instead quietly communed with it as Edie looked on. After several minutes the figure darted away, and they continued on their way. I feel certain that Choiya has come to our family to play an integral part in our experiment with the Devas here on this land. She keeps us on our toes and teaches us constantly to pay attention to the slightest impressions. Machaelle Small Wright reminds us that "the key to working with the Devic realm is our willingness to act on impression."

One of our early experiences in the spiral garden was with the deer, who rarely walk across our land because the dogs bark at them. They tend to stay in the woods on the edge of the fields and gardens. This particular morning was crystal clear, with the spring warmth inviting the plants to burst forth. Amy and I were sitting in the center of the spiral garden. We were dedicating ourselves to working with the Devas, the elementals, the insects, the animals, and all our relations on this sweet piece of earth. Since we were relatively new to this type of work, we were asking for guidance and understanding in how to incorporate a co-creative partnership into a working farm. We also were struggling with what I call the internal nag: that part of yourself that doubts everything. Amy, especially, was wondering how in the world we were having a partnership with something we couldn't see. I implored her to trust that this was the direction for us to take to bring balance back to this piece of land. We spent several minutes quieting ourselves, focusing, and listening. At a certain moment, we simultaneously opened our eyes to see two deer standing at the edge of the garden no more than thirty feet from us. They stood motionless for quite some time, staring unwaveringly into our eyes. Their soft brown eyes invited us to soften and feel what our hearts were telling us. We were given a clear impression from the deer—which we could see—that the direction we were headed in was exactly what needed to happen. This was the affirmation we needed to dive into co-creative partnership with a passion. We've never seen deer in or near the gardens since.

Animals' keen sensibilities give them a way of knowing when to be there for humans. Cathy tells of a time when she needed a boost of reassurance in her work as a Reiki practitioner:

> After I received my second degree in Reiki I was walking up the mountain early one morning. It was quite foggy. As I came around a bend I saw two deer, a mother and her baby. I stopped and made one of my symbols (Reiki) and held my hand up to let the baby draw energy if she wanted it. The fawn came closer and closer. Suddenly, to my right I heard (in my mind—I think) "Look, she has the light!" It didn't come from the deer, and my sense was it was the little people. In this same spot I was also gifted with a beautiful turkey feather. It was not there on my way up the mountain, but on my way down I found it directly in my path wedged in between two rocks. I felt this was a gift left for me.

The deer gave Cathy the opportunity to use her Reiki, and the "little people" confirmed that she indeed had what it took to be effective. The gift of the turkey feather was the physical manifestation of the affirmation given to her to pursue her Reiki work. Each time she looks at the turkey feather or uses it in her work, she is reminded of her light and healing powers.

While on vision quest in Montana, Chris had an experience that was undeniably a powerful helping hand from an animal ally. She had gone to high ground overlooking the beautiful Blacktail valley with the Continental Divide in the distance. Here she made her circle and prayed for her vision. About halfway into the first day, a large snake crawled into her circle and quietly made itself at home. We are taught prior to going out on quest to ask for only what is needed for our growth to enter our circle. What doesn't serve us is asked to not enter our sacred space. Chris had never been in such close proximity to such a large snake, and, quite frankly, she was a little afraid of snakes. But it wasn't bothering her, and she trusted that this was exactly what her vision quest was about. Over the next two days, the snake shed its skin right in front of her eyes. Chris spent the time spellbound by the snake and the transformation it was going through. She saw that her life was in need of major transformation and that she needed to shed the worn-out skin, that part of her life that no longer served her. Chris returned to camp with her snakeskin, vowing to change her life and pursue her passions. She enrolled at the California School of Herbal Studies and began to learn about the healing qualities of plants, fulfilling a dream she'd had for quite some time. We may ask: How did this snake know to crawl into her circle and shed its skin in front of her? Is this part of the universal intelligence that Linda Tellington-Jones speaks of?

Mary refers to this intelligence in another way:

> One morning I was hurrying through my routine, just wanting to get all my little chores done so I could get out to work. I always give Pansy, my cat, flower essences to keep her urinary tract clear of blockages, as she has real problems otherwise. So I was just rushing along giving her the essences, my mind far away. As I put the drops in her mouth, I looked into Pansy's eyes and I was amazed. I felt as if I were looking into God's eyes. It was as if all of God looked out at me, so infinitely wise, so aware of me. It was as if the entire universe was there in that consciousness. Many times I've looked, but I've never been treated to that again. Perhaps the message was that although I may think that Pansy is "just my cat," she is actually an expression of God, as are all living beings, and should be treated with tenderness and respect and that it really matters how I treat her.

When we see this Lumelligence as a piece of God, we begin to view the world differently. We realize that all our relatives' Lumelligence, as well as our own, is a piece of the Great Spirit. We begin to see the divinity that resides in all beings as our common union.

Animals often have strong messages for us. If we take the time to listen, we are richly rewarded by their desire to help us. I experienced my friend and ally the Hummingbird the year after my vision quest, again at Blacktail Ranch. This time I was at Blacktail not as a camper but as a teacher. Shortly after arriving, I became ill with intense diarrhea. I was at one of Brooke's camps to teach about Devas, flower essences, and the spirit alive in all of life, especially at Blacktail. I wasn't quite sure how I was going to pull it together to teach when I was feeling so terrible. After about three days of this, I finally decided to stop eating, thus ending the diarrhea. I was to give an evening presentation on co-creative partnership and didn't want to run out to the outhouse every few minutes. As I stepped outside of my tent, there was a hummingbird hovering very close to me. I was delighted to see her again. I wasn't quite sure what this visit was about, but I waited. Much to my amazement, she landed on the branch of a bush only five feet away and sat very still. I had never seen a hummingbird sit still before. She sat for a very long time while I stood staring at her. I took this special opportunity to move into vibrational resonance with her and meet her on that common ground. She assured me not to be afraid, despite my old fear of birds. She said that it was imperative for me to be very clear about the information I was sharing with the folks at camp. I had been carrying some emotional garbage that needed releasing before I could be clear for the teaching. Well, that explained the diarrhea. The hummingbird helped me in that moment to breathe into the place of holding and let it drain out the bottom of my feet into the earth, where the energy was neutralized. I could have stayed there all night with her, but I had to get going for the evening teaching session. I thanked her for her help and went on to have a great time at camp that year, playing with the Devas and all my Eagle Song sisters. Since then, hummingbirds come to my kitchen window frequently. I plant Mexican sunflowers right by the window so they have beautiful flowers to enjoy. I no longer panic when I see them so near, knowing that they are coming to serve as my ally and to remind me of the joyful side of life.

When we approach animals in a conscious way, we can live in harmony with them again. A great example of this is the Phoenicia Pathwork Center, in the Catskill Mountains, where we hold an annual herbal conference called the Green Nations Gathering. The community of people who live there are co-creatively partnering with the wildlife all around them. The deer at the Center are treated with the utmost respect. They know that no one will harm them, so they calmly graze along the pathways even when the Center is full of people. It is so reassuring to see people and animals co-existing in such a peaceful way. An ancient memory rises in me when I stretch my hand out to a yearling deer to have it nibble an apple from my palm.

ANIMALS AND FLOWER ESSENCES

Because of animals' strong sensitivities to energy, they have a particular affinity to the healing powers of flower essences. When Kate was preparing for her move from Massachusetts to New York, she became increasingly concerned about the family cat, Milkweed. She had had cats in the past that became completely traumatized by a move and ran away once moved to unfamiliar territory. Milkweed, like most cats, was very uncomfortable traveling in a car. Kate decided, initially, to give her cat Rescue Remedy, a Bach Flower Essence combination used during any trauma, to help him handle the car ride. When they arrived at their new place, she began giving him Quaking Aspen and Hemlock flower essence along with the Rescue Remedy. Quaking Aspen is specifically used for fear of the unknown, and Hemlock is used for any big change or transformation. The first day Milkweed spent his time exploring every nook and cranny of the new house on the inside. The second day he walked the perimeter of the house outside, sniffing, digging, and sensing the environs. By the third day he was completely at home without one bit of trauma or confusion. Milkweed had slipped into his new scene easily with the aid of flower essences.

⁂

Mary uses flower essences often with her cats. One evening her cat, Emily, began having some sort of attack. Her mouth was open, her gums were pale and she was panting rapidly. Mary knew immediately to give the cat Rescue Remedy. She asked Emily what was happening to her. Mary felt deep pains in her heart. She knew that Emily was having a heart attack. Again she asked Emily how she could best help her in that moment. She was directed to put the Rescue Remedy on Emily's paws, and Emily licked it off. She continued putting the essences on her paws until Emily became calm and breathing was normal. Emily had been having attacks for quite some time, and not until then did Mary know why. Emily's heart had become so weakened that she was unable to continue living. She died that weekend. Mary's other cat, Pansy, was so stricken with grief over the loss of Emily that she wouldn't eat or be active. Mary gave her Sweet Chestnut for grief and Honeysuckle for letting go of the past. In less than a week, Pansy was back to normal.

*

Deb likes to combine flower essences with herbal or homeopathic remedies. She feels that this approach offers a broader range of healing. One morning she was called by a friend who lived about an hour from her house. The friend knew she had been looking for a kitten, and a small kitten had been dropped on the road and was now living near her compost pile, eating the food scraps that were dumped there. Through offerings of food and telepathic communication, Deb's friend was able to coax the kitten into a box. Deb took in Max when he was about two months old. When he arrived at her house he was terrified. He was so frightened that he ran and hid between two walls in a room that was off of the main portion of the house. She put a bowl of milk containing Rescue Remedy and Aconite (a homeopathic remedy given for fear) near the wall he was hiding in. She would talk in a quiet soothing voice to the kitten and send mental images to welcome Max to his new home. Each day there was less milk in the bowl. By the third day, Max was walking around the room and Deb was able to hold him. Within a week the traumatized kitten felt completely at home.

*

Hart reminds me that it's not always necessary for animals to ingest flower essences. She had a goat named Lucy who had aborted and was having a difficult time coming back into heat. Hart felt she was having a hard time letting go of the trauma of aborting. She poured Great Angelica essence down her spine, and Lucy immediately calmed down and within a few hours began to go into heat.

*

Debbie is a riding instructor and holistic health practitioner with horses. She uses flower essences both alone and in combination with herbal preparations for her horses and her students' horses. She made a believer out of one of her students when she recommended using Rescue Remedy on Tres, her student's horse. He was experiencing pain, and Debbie wanted to show the difference in how Tres would perform when not in pain. They gave him the Rescue Remedy, and immediately there was a marked difference in his ability to "move out." Once the Rescue Remedy wore off, he went back to resisting. Debbie's student was amazed at the difference. She decided to work with Tres in other areas, using the flower essences. She had a sense that his spirit had been broken while he was racing at the track. He had developed an independent attitude as a survival mechanism, and he was rather depressed. He was given Rock Water flower essence to help him lighten up and Dandelion essence to help loosen up his muscles. He responded well to the essences and is now on his way to a happier, healthier life.

Debbie has also noticed that changes in weather—from fair to stormy or warm to cold—can affect horses. Their backs actually go out, and this adversely affects their performance. For example, they may have trouble getting the correct lead change when their backs are out. Debbie has gotten quick results from using combinations of herbs and flower essences to remedy this problem. She administers the flower essences by putting them in a little water and then squirting it in their mouths with a spray bottle or syringe.

✼

I had another amazing communion with the animal kingdom while doing a workshop at Kate's place at the edge of the Adirondack Park in New York. We were teaching people about flower essences, and each person was making their own essence. I was working on a new set of essences to use in homecoming healings and with healing the split between abused relatives and humans. I had seen a knapweed plant on the road while we were walking earlier, and I'd had a strong pull to work with knapweed for some time. I was happy to have the opportunity to begin partnering with a new friend. Full of anticipation, I walked down the road with my glass bowl and spring water. I asked to be connected to the Knapweed Deva and allowed myself to move into the same vibrational resonance. I saw knapweed and how it had begun to grow prolifically in many areas to the point of almost taking over an entire area. Its stalk is woody and quite strong, and it has tenacious roots that are not easily pulled from the ground. This plant is a survivor. I dropped down one more level and looked into the essence of the plant. Here was a plant that would survive no matter what measures were taken to eradicate it. This would never become an endangered species. It tends to grow where civilization has encroached, sometimes to an extreme extent. Is it trying to put the wild back into the environment? As I traveled inside myself as knapweed, I began to feel a little nag at me. I had been gone quite awhile, and, since I was one of the teachers, it was probably a good idea for me to not be late in returning to share about our flowers.

I pulled myself out of my communion and headed back up the road, vowing to work more with knapweed by taking the essence I had made. Now I was feeling very rushed, needing to get back. I hurried up the road, deep in thought about my experience with knapweed, passed a small grassy lane that entered the road on the right, and smiled as I noticed the sign "Partridge Lane." Did partridge still stroll up that lane? I kept up my brisk pace and was approaching the top of the hill when I heard a very loud, deep grunt. What was that! The sound made me stop dead in my tracks. I slowly turned around to see a black bear standing up on its hind legs looking straight at me. A streak of fear ran through me, and then I remembered to take a deep breath. This was a relative of mine that I had rarely encountered, and here in this moment I was given the opportunity to exchange energy with it. It seemed the bear had called to me to get my attention and then stood up so I would see it clearly. We held each other's gaze for some time, and then I looked down at the Knapweed essence in my hand. What was the connection between the two? I connected with the Bear Deva and asked how the essence could interact with it. It became perfectly clear to me in that moment that Knapweed essence was to be used to heal the split with wild animals and wild places that had been encroached upon by modern civilization. I thanked my ally the bear and then shifted my energy, preparing to leave. The bear dropped down on all fours and began to amble toward me. Very slowly, I backed up, still looking at the bear and then turned and walked on, once I reached the top of the hill. So ecstatic about this experience that I could hardly contain myself, I hurried back to the group and excitedly told my story. Joyce, at whose home we were holding our class, calmly said, "Bear Spirit is with you." She, being a member of the Bear Clan of the Mohawk Nation, recognized that I had been touched by the bear.

As I reflected on Bear energy I remembered being in the cave at Blacktail Ranch in Montana. In this cave, where the only Kodiak bear skull in the lower forty-eight states was found, it is said that a Bear shaman lived and taught his apprentices. The first time I was filled with Bear essence was while visiting the cave with a group of women from Brooke Medicine Eagle's Eagle Song Vision Quest Camp. The group was circled in the large cavern where the Bear shaman lived. The lights were turned out, and it was so dark I couldn't see my hand in front of my face. I had never been in such darkness. All was silent except for the drip-drip of water, keeping this inner world moist and juicy. I was truly in the womb of the earth. Then came the sounds of low growls, shuffling, and grunting. My whole being stiffened, and I listened breathlessly. A shot of fear ran up my back. Was this how the Bear shaman began with his apprentices? I calmed myself and began to take long, slow breaths. I asked to be connected to the Bear Deva. She shared with me the essence of Bear, which is feminine and wild. She also showed me the dreamtime and how with Bear energy the dreamtime can be accessed so that it can help us understand other dimensions. I let my mind go and dropped into the feeling sense of my body. Here I found the deep feminine inside myself. It was soft and warm, yet wet and wild. I traveled into the caverns of my being, finding my way home. I emerged from the cave that day knowing I had been profoundly touched but not fully realizing how the experience would be manifested. It wasn't until I met the bear face to face at Adirondack Park that I grasped the extent of my kinship with the bear. Bear helps me to know my feminine self in the deepest way and through this knowingness be able to bring balance to an overly masculine, tamed, and logical world.

One of my favorite authors, Terry Tempest Williams, speaks of bears in her book *An Unspoken Hunger:*

> I believe in the power of Bear. The Feminine has long been linked to the bear through mythology. The Greek goddess Artemis, whose name means "bear," embodies the wisdom of the wild . . . . By undressing, exposing, and embracing the bear, we undress, expose, and embrace our authentic selves. Stripped free from society's oughts and shoulds, we emerge as emancipated beings. The bear is free to roam.

Bear has become my ally as I strive to be in co-creative partnership with all my relations. When I doubt or falter, I connect with Bear Deva and I remember myself.

PARTNERING WITH ANIMALS

In ancient cultures, animals were treated as brothers and sisters. It was understood that without them the cycle of life could not continue. Native people relied heavily on them for food, clothing, housing, and other useful items. When food was needed, the shaman of the tribe would call an animal in and then merge with the soul of the animal. He would explain the needs of his tribe for food, and a mutual agreement would be made for the animal to give of his life so the people could live. The shaman would assist the animal's soul in leaving his body so that a smooth transition to the "other world" could be made. The exchange was made only if there was agreement by the animal. The people knew that if they took the life of an animal that was not willing to give of itself, they might disrupt the balance, and hunting of animals would become more difficult. This very deep communion with animals took place for centuries. Now, animals are not only treated disrespectfully but tortured with deplorable living conditions and shot full of growth hormones to speed their development or make more milk or plop out more eggs. We have become so disconnected from the source of our food that we no longer realize that the fat steak at the supermarket was once a cow with soft brown eyes, feelings, and intelligence.

Scott and I always raised our own meat, feeling that we wanted to raise our animals with love and kill them in a respectful way. We felt the meat was much healthier for us when it was produced in this way. Scott would shoot the animals in the head to stun them, and then slit their throats and let the blood drain out. It sounds gruesome, but it was actually the least traumatizing way to give death.

It was hog butchering time, and we were preparing Pork Chop to become exactly that. This time when Scott shot Pork Chop, the hog reared back, let out a scream, and then struggled violently to tear himself away from our grasp. Scott had to shoot him twice more before the animal was calm enough to have his throat slit. It was one of the most traumatic experiences I'd ever had with an animal. This pig did not want to die, and yet we were forcing death upon him. Where was my respect now? I realized in that moment how animals' lives were being taken all the time without the least bit of respect, understanding, or communication of humans' intentions. My relationship with Pork Chop had only been superficial. I still was the almighty one dominating the situation. I had left out the key ingredient which was to make sure it was OK with Pork Chop that he give of himself for us. In that moment I vowed to become partners with the animals I was in contact with. I also knew that eating meat was no longer nourishing me on a soul level and that I had to let go of it to move into a co-creative partnership with animals.

Partnering with animals other than domesticated ones is not always that easy. Insects and rodents are particularly challenging because they have been perceived as the enemy for so long. With the animal kingdom, compromise is often the key to bringing balance to a situation. The first summer we lived in the tipi we had a dirt floor with little covering. By midsummer, when it was dry and sweltering hot the tipi would be cooled by the shaded earthen floor. One day I walked into the tipi and found it covered with little centipede-type worms. They were everywhere—on the inside walls, the bed, the dresser, the floor. There were so many that they crunched under my feet as I walked into the tipi. I connected with the Deva of these worms and asked for them to leave. The next day they were still there. Obviously, something else needed to happen besides my imploring them to go somewhere else. This time I allowed myself to drop into their vibratory level to get a deeper understanding of their presence in the tipi. It became obvious to me that the reason they were there was that it was one of the few places that provided them protection from the heat. They liked the cool dirt floor of the tipi. I explained that this was my living space and that I needed to walk around in here—which was not so good for them—and that my bed was really only for me, not for them. I also let them know that my intention was not to kill them but that we needed to work something out that was mutually acceptable. I had to be the one to find the workable compromise, since I was the one having a hard time with their presence. I asked them to please not get in my bed and suggested that it would be best to stay along the edges instead of the middle of the tipi so they wouldn't get crushed. The next day I went into the tipi and there were no worms in the bed and only a few here and there in the middle of the tipi. The compromise had worked: we both were able to get what we needed without aggression.

On another occasion during a particularly cold winter we had rats living in the greenhouse. The rat issue is always a bone of contention between Amy and me. She still can't "get" co-existing with them. The reality is that we live along a river where there will always be rats. Anyway, this particular winter a large crew of them moved into the greenhouse. It was getting close to the time to plant seeds, so Amy wanted to know what I was going to do about the rats. She said, "You better get out there and start talkin'; this may take a while." In the meantime, we had gone to Cara's riding stable, where the owners had a wild tomcat they wanted to get rid of. Amy jumped at the chance to put a cat in the greenhouse. I was not keen on the idea because I hadn't had a chance to talk to the rats yet. After much chasing, we finally caught the cat and brought it home. In less than two days, the cat left, never to be seen again. I had never worked with rats before, so I wasn't quite sure what I was in for. I went to the greenhouse, settled myself in, and asked to be connected to the Rat Deva. I explained our situation—that we needed to start planting soon—and said I wanted to work something out that would be mutually beneficial. The energy that came through was a bit indignant. The understanding through my felt sense was, "Why did you bring that cat in here if you wanted to work something out? It seems to me you wanted to kill us." I immediately apologized and said it really wasn't my idea and that ultimately we both wanted to find a peaceful agreement. It then became clear to me what the rats needed. The snows were melting and it was warming up outside, so

Photograph by Cara Montgomery

the cold was no longer a factor, but they wouldn't have food still for awhile. I asked if they would be willing to move out of the greenhouse into the brush pile at the edge of the property if I fed them. From then until spring I sprinkled seeds and nuts along the edge of the property, and there were no more rats in the greenhouse. After about three weeks of working in the greenhouse, I asked Amy if she had noticed anything. She said how nice the new little parsley sprouts looked. I told her that was not what I meant. She paused a moment and then said, "How did you do that? Where'd the rats go?" I told her what I had done. She was happy to not have the rats in the greenhouse, but I must admit that she thinks I'm a little wacky to feed rats. I'm able to do this because my intention is to live in a co-creative environment where all of life is respected for the part it plays in the vast web of interconnected relations.

Since the time of feeding the rats I've come to a deeper understanding of the balance and the imbalance on the earth. The natural rhythm and cycle has been so disrupted that sometimes we humans have to play the predator role. Amy came to me one day and said, "Please come out here and listen to these poor roses. They are crying for relief from these aphids." I could see how depleted they looked and did feel their anxiety. Amy begged me to let her kill the aphids. She explained to me that the natural predator–prey relationship had been so disrupted by the use of chemicals on apple farms in the Hudson Valley that it was impossible for the balance to occur naturally. I saw in that moment that we as humans need, at times, to become predators, but that the way in which we approach the aphids makes all the difference in the world. If we carry a warring energy and have the attitude, "I'm going to get you, you little suckers," that is very different from an attitude of respect and clear intention to bring balance. I told Amy it was OK to kill them as long as she communicated her intentions to them. She did this, and the entire area in front of the house where the roses were growing lightened. The roses were so grateful to be relieved of the aphid burden that they bloomed and bloomed and bloomed that season.

While I sit here writing, my cat, Honeycat, sits with his paws across my chest and purrs loudly. Every now and then he will stretch out a paw and touch my face or lift his face to mine and rub against my cheek. He is so unconditionally devoted to dwelling in the love vibration that when I'm around him I can not deny its existence and its effects. He keeps me focused in the energy field of love as I write and reminds me that this place is where true healing and transformation takes place. As I look into his eyes I can hardly believe that only a short three hundred years ago this animal was still wild. Can we overcome our fear of most of the animal kingdom by recognizing them as very close relatives, even in their wildness? We can begin to heal the split with all the animals by connecting with the Devas of the animals and taking flower essences to help us transform our fearful energy into loving, respectful kinship. With time the trust will return, and our family will broaden to include not only cats, dogs, and horses but bears, mountain lions, wolves, and whales.

7

HOMECOMING HEALINGS

When we look at all aspects of nature as being our relatives, we see what a large family we are. We also see how distant we have become from some of our relatives. Some we barely know, and others we have downright abused. In order for us to move on the evolutionary spiral, it is time to bring all our relations back into the family circle. To heal the splits with these abused relatives we must consciously work from a place of equality, not dominion, to be in a co-creative partnership. We must strive to view the world as a both/and place—rather than either/or—where each and every creature, stone, plant, waterway, piece of dirt, mineral, tree, landscape, and every other relative has a rightful place in the whole. We must also see that without one of these relatives the entire balance shifts and changes, thus affecting the whole.

To restore balance with abused relatives I have been doing what I call homecoming healings. The idea is to heal the split with abused relatives and bring them back into the family fold or invite them home. It is a conscious act of communion, usually aided by flower essences; prayer; vibrational resonance like singing, drumming, rattling; or sometimes just connecting through my heart and pouring all my love into my relative. Some type of action is usually required for the healing to be fully complete. However, once a co-creative partnership begins, there is a continual ongoing relationship that never ends.

Photograph by Pam Montgomery

One of the major relatives in my life is the Hudson River, which runs right in front of my home. Because this relative is a constant presence and we are dedicated to co-creative partnership with all of life at our place, Amy and I decided we needed to do healing work with the Hudson. We went to the river at the Spring Equinox and each took Borage essence, which specifically partners with water elements, and we gave the essence to the River as well. I connected with the Deva of the Hudson River and allowed myself to feel the fullness of this majestic body of water. I felt myself move with the tide that flows up the Hudson from the Atlantic Ocean being pulled with a force not all my own but more primal and celestial. I tasted the hint of salt on my lips, reminding me further of the river's ocean origins. I felt the sun on my surface, creating sparkling patterns of light, dancing with every wave. I rolled with the waves of motion, feeling the awesomeness of water and its place on this earth. I felt the waters inside myself and how without them I would not live. I swam deep within my inner waters, searching for the place of separation. I realized that even though I admired the Hudson for her great beauty I also carried an aversion to her because of my belief that the Hudson is polluted. I could enjoy her from a distance and swim in her waters in my mind, but I would never actually put my body in her. I told the Deva of the Hudson that this was the place I needed to heal. She responded by saying, "Do you stop loving a child because it is handicapped, or a sister when she gets cancer, or a parent who becomes old and less capable, or a friend who loses a limb? Why then would you stop loving me because I've become polluted by the acts of another?" This insight hit me at the core of my being, and I saw clearly that I had treated the river as a lessor being because it was polluted. I vowed in that moment to heal the split with the Hudson River, knowing that her waters will never run clean and clear if I continue to carry the energy of disgust because of pollution. When I swim in her waters instead of worrying about what the polluted waters are doing to me, I will rejoice in knowing that my love is healing her and through this act of partnering I, too, will become rejuvenated and whole.

I now have Hudson River water in a special bowl in my house. Each day I anoint myself with her, treating her as holy water, and I say a prayer for her health. I have a vision of going aboard the *Clearwater* boat, dedicated to cleaning up the Hudson, sharing a homecoming healing with all the crew members, anointing them with the holy waters of the Hudson. From then on, all the people who board the *Clearwater* will be anointed with the holy water of the Hudson, and scores of people will begin to see the river as clean, whole, and balanced again. Someday she indeed will run clear and pure.

On another occasion, I had the opportunity to begin healing the split with one more water relative and all its beings while doing a workshop in Provincetown on Cape Cod. We had spent the weekend learning about co-creative partnership and how to communicate with the devic realm. Because we were surrounded by the ocean we felt that it was appropriate to partner with her and all her beings. It was spring and not exactly beach weather, but we decided to go to the beach anyway. We bundled up in our winter coats and hats and headed off. I had brought with me my crystal bowl and was inspired to bring it to the beach. There were only a few other people on the beach because the weather was so gray and drizzly. We began by playing the crystal bowl and allowing ourselves to move into aspects of the ocean. Each one of us became an ocean creature or element. One person was a whale, another a manatee, another a seal, another seaweed, and so on. I was the ocean herself. After moving into resonance with each of our ocean selves, we held a council of ocean beings. Each person spoke as if he or she was the ocean being itself. We spoke of our existence as ocean beings. We spoke of the hurts inflicted upon us and how it affected us. We spoke of what we needed to heal the splits with our human relatives. As each of us spoke, the rest of the group gave witness to our plight. We were heard and our voices were acknowledged with deep respect. We completed our council with commitments to consciously partner with the ocean and all her beings and to actively work to bring balance to this awesome relative. We then each took Jasmine essence and gave some to the ocean. I had made this essence while in Vieques, Puerto Rico, and had been told to give it to the oceans of the world. The clouds opened briefly, and a direct beam of light shone on us as we performed our ritual. We lined up along the beach to offer our final prayers, and there off the shoreline was a large finback whale breaching out of the water right in front of us. We all gasped in amazement. Our communion was not only heard but acknowledged through direct contact by one of the relatives we partnered with. One of our group members, Marsha, was a whale and dolphin researcher, and she told us that finback whales are the second largest whale in the world. We all felt humbled by the experience and in that moment realized how important our conscious communications and healing intentions are. We had gone beyond the confines of our limited perception of the world and viewed life through the eyes of others. For this we were richly rewarded.

While in Montana I began to heal the split with tobacco, another relative that has been terribly abused. Tobacco and cornmeal are both used during morning prayers at vision quest camp, and I always felt myself just going through the motions of using them without really feeling the essence of their being and its effect on my prayers. I carried the belief that tobacco was harmful to your health when smoked and was therefore bad. I had never stopped to think about its true nature and realize that it wasn't tobacco's fault that humans were taking advantage of its powerful effects on the body. It wasn't until my Eagle Song sister, Mary, helped me to understand the essence of tobacco that I began to heal the split with this most wonderful relative. She told me that tobacco has the ability to carry the spirit essence of all our relations and that when we pray with tobacco we are bridging the world of spirit and form. Tobacco was never intended to be used recreationally. It is a powerful plant that is intended for ceremonial use or for prayer. The tremendous abuse that has been placed on this plant is almost incomprehensible. I vowed to change my relationship to tobacco and begin to partner with it through prayer and communion.

I acquired a tobacco pouch on this particular trip to Montana and filled it with tobacco. I prayed every day with tobacco, letting the spirit of all my relations be infused in my prayers. I tied the pouch to my jeans and carried it with me wherever I went. I offered tobacco to plants I was working with, to people I encountered, to animals whose path I crossed, to rocks and streams. I immersed myself in tobacco and its essence. Tobacco has become a medicine plant ally that guides and shapes, through prayer, many of my interactions with my relatives. Now I grow my own tobacco in order to infuse it with love and gratitude as it grows, so that when I use it later it is that much more powerful. Tobacco has taught me that nothing is to go unnoticed. Everything is worthy of prayer and gratitude. A simple pinch of tobacco can acknowledge the kinship with all of life and enhance co-creative partnership.

My vision for bringing all my relatives back home again is extensive. To some this work may seem all in the spirit realm—as my friend Doug says, "All that airy-fairy stuff." It's not just airy-fairy but also earthy-humany. The two combine to co-create. The whole point is to manifest in a way that is nondestructive to the earth. By paying attention and listening to our relatives, by consciously working together as equal partners, by recognizing intelligent light energy, and by being grateful for our connection to all of life, we can evolve on this planet to a place of balance and peace.

One way this is manifesting is the work of an organization called United Plant Savers. Together with the Northeast Herbal Association we did a replanting project at the Phoenicia Pathwork Center, where we planted two hundred goldenseal rootlets in the woods. Before we began individually planting our rootlets, we offered a prayer for their healthy growth and for the woods to accept them into its ecology. We were instructed how to properly plant a root and where and how goldenseal particularly likes to grow. I cradled my little goldenseal roots in my hand and asked to be connected to the Lumelligence of Goldenseal. I felt the strength of this powerful medicinal plant and its gratitude for being reintroduced into woods where it once flourished. I was drawn to a small rise in the earth near the stream. Here, with healing intent for the earth and goldenseal, I planted my rootlets in a circle. I prayed that they might flourish undisturbed and that one day they would be grandmother plants. Through the work of United Plant Savers we educate people to the dangers of overharvesting medicinal wild plants and conduct replanting projects throughout the country to increase the populations of endangered species or those that are being threatened by abundant use and loss of habitat. We are listening to our medicine plant relatives as they become alarmed by unconscious harvesting, and we are bringing them home again before it's too late.

My visions carry me to all parts of the world where abused relatives live. I see the clear-cut rainforests in their nakedness crying out to not be stripped of their dignity anymore. I see the hollow shell of a uranium mine, its powerful pulse only an echo. I see the underwater world of the South Pacific, where the nuclear bomb testing explodes fish, coral, dolphins, seaweed, and creatures of all kinds into a million little pieces. I see the fields of the Midwestern Great Plains being monocropped to death, leaving the once fertile soil like a ghost that disappears with the wind. These are the places I want to go to create homecoming healings. I see small groups of people coming together to heal the split with our abused relatives. As few as twelve people coming together with focused intent and directed energy can have a resulting magnitude of force that is not the same as twelve individuals working alone. It is the force of a multitude. In my vision I see all shapes and types and colors of people from many different backgrounds. I see no exclusiveness because of race, religion, or economic standing. Being a very practical person (Sun in Taurus with a Capricorn Moon), I realize that these homecoming healings will need resources in order to be accomplished, thus the establishment of the Partner Earth Education Center. Is this just a fantasy dream to cope with a world gone mad, or is the reality that because I can think it, PEEC can be possible?

HOLDING THE CIRCLE THROUGH CEREMONY

The pagan revival has brought ceremony and ritual back into our lives. Despite some Christians' belief that paganism is devil-worship, the word *pagan* means "of the country" and has nothing to do with the devil, nor is there any idolatry of a false God. Neopagans recognize the spirit in all life and acknowledge it through ceremonial celebration. The seasons are honored, the moon cycles and their effects are felt, and rites of passage are commemorated. This celebration of life is done in a joyful manner with the intent to connect with Partner Earth and all her beings. Each time a celebration of Partner Earth takes place, it reverberates through every fiber of the planet with the vibration of "Yes!" This vibration carries the frequency of love, joy, and gratitude. It is then mirrored back to us in a million different ways through inspiring encounters with one of our relatives: a beautiful sunset, a peaceful moment at a waterfall, or an eagle soaring overhead. It can also manifest in other ways, like a helping hand from a friend, a peace treaty in Bosnia, or an overdue rainfall in Africa.

Brooke Medicine Eagle tells us that the Native American elders who have been holding the sacred circle together for centuries can no longer do this for all of us. It is time for us to take the responsibility of creating our own ceremonies to mend the web and walk in the circle of life. It is important to incorporate drumming, dancing, singing, and chanting into ceremony. It's essential to remember that our ceremonies are celebrations of the spirit and sacredness in all life.

During vision quest camp at Blacktail Ranch, the staff members drum for the campers while they are out on quest. This is a ritual way of holding the energy while they are seeking a vision. On one particular occasion, it was nighttime and we were in the yurt, a structure used traditionally by nomadic people, with the big Mother Drum. We began with a slow rhythmical drumming as we visualized each camper and the spot where each was questing. We tuned into each of our sisters and sent energy where it was needed. Just as we were finishing with the campers, the wind picked up. Our drumming pace increased with the wind. The sky began to light up and the energy rose. We each took on an individual beat and yet were in complete harmony. Rain began to fall, blessing the earth with its life-giving force. The wind blew harder and our drumming rhythm increased. The lightning flashing in the sky was visible through the skylight dome of the yurt. We sat, one in each of the four directions, with Partner Earth under us, the sky above us, and Mother Drum at our center. We drummed furiously as the rain poured down, the wind whipped, and the lightning bolts lit up our drum.

It was as if the elements were in complete harmonious sound resonance with us. There was no separation between us, the wind, the rain, the lightning, and the drum. We reveled in the bliss of this ecstatic communion. This was one of the most awesome experiences I've ever had while drumming. The drum was inside me. I knew exactly how to beat it to create perfect resonance. Through this ritual act I had helped my sisters, moved in harmony with the elements, and co-creatively partnered with Mother Drum. The vibration produced by the blending of all these energies was profoundly healing for Partner Earth, the questers, myself, and my drum partners.

Again in Montana, this time on the banks of the Blackfoot River, we gathered at the Summer Solstice to celebrate the longest day of the year—the time in the cycle of seasons when we are filled with the most amount of light. We picked a tree on the property we were all attracted to, to serve as our center point of focus and to represent the Tree of Life. We began by calling in the seven directions. There were seven of us, and each took a direction. The powers of the East were called: spirits of the sunrise, new beginnings, and illumination, the abilities of far-sightedness, home of the Eagle. The powers of the South were called: spirits of bright light, warmth, playfulness and joy, the abilities of trust and innocence, home of the Mouse and Coyote. The powers of the West were called: spirits of the sunset and twilight when the veil between the worlds is thin, the "looks within" place of deep introspection, home of the Bear and Crow. The powers of the North were called: the spirits of the night and crystalline silence, the abilities of wisdom and universal knowing, home of the Buffalo and Owl. The powers of the Above were called: Sky beings, winged ones, celestial and cosmic forces, and spirits of heaven. The powers of Below were called: Earth beings, creepy crawlies, four-leggeds, two-leggeds, and spirits of the subterranean. The powers of the Center were called: the one-heart place where we all reside. We then stated our intention for our ceremony, which was to honor the sun, be in communion with all of life, take responsibility for our part in mending the hoop, contribute to Earth health, acknowledge our Beauty Way, and give thanks to all our relations. We created an altar around the base of the tree by placing special stones, objects, and feathers that held meaning for each of us. We then danced and drummed around the Tree of Life, calling all into the circle. We called not only the bear, deer, wolf, and eagle, the plants both edible and medicinal, the beautiful flowers, the moon, the stars, the crystals and waters but also government leaders, nuclear power plants, viruses, pesticides, and fossil fuels. We embraced all of life and prayed for the healing of all relations within the vast web of creation. We became the weavers, mending tears within the energetic fabric of reality. Our dance went on and on well into the afternoon. We ran to the center and gathered energy from the Tree of Life and at the same time gave prayers for specific healing that needed to take place. Our day was filled with continual prayer and thanksgiving.

The next day we spent the morning quietly walking the land, listening to our relatives, and choosing stones of graduated size for our sun wheel dance. At high noon we gathered around a large tree stump that was the center of our sun. We each laid out the rocks we had gathered, starting with the biggest in the center and working our way out in rays from the center, ending with the smallest stone. We danced and rattled around and around the center, then in and out each of our rays. We danced for the life-giving force of the sun, and we prayed to be filled with light. For hours we danced until we were in a trance, moving through the motions but in another dimension, riding the waves of light emanating from the sun. At the end of our dance, Marion shared the song that had been given to her while dancing:

Thank you that I might be like you,
catching the light, holding the light, sharing the light,
giving light back to life.

We felt the fullness of the day and let it spill from our hearts in joyful song.

That evening we ended our Solstice celebration with a pipe ceremony led by Heron. She filled the pipe with several pinches of tobacco, each representing one of our relations. The last pinch was for all relations not mentioned, so we would not miss anyone. Jamie Sams says of the Pipe Ceremony:

> We find union with All Our Relations when we share the Pipe. The essence of every living creature enters us when we smoke them and we carry their spirits inside our bodies. We are reminded that harmony is attained through sacred union with all our fellow beings. We never place the spirit of any life-form outside of ourselves since through the Pipe, we have asked them to enter our being and share our Sacred Space and life experience.

The smoking of the pipe that night was the perfect ending to a glorious two days of prayer, thanksgiving, dance, and celebration. I rejoice in the remembrance of conscious committed praying for Partner Earth and all my relations.

RESACRALIZING PARTNER EARTH

Centuries ago, Partner Earth's power spots were recognized and sacred space was created at these places. A power spot can be where energy lines intersect or where portals to other dimensions are located. The Medicine Rocks are just such a place that served as a natural Earth altar for the people. The people recognized this spot as a place with great healing power and honored it by giving offerings of both prayer and objects. There are many sacred sites around the planet that were once held in reverence and now are merely tourist attractions. The loss of sacred space has contributed to the desensitization of Partner Earth. It is important for us to create sacred space again in order to gain a new intimacy with Partner Earth.

Photograph by Pam Montgomery

One way we can create sacred space is to make gardens, no matter how small they might be. A garden is a place to love, nourish, and honor the miracle of life. Each time I put a seed in the ground I'm in awe of the magnificent plant that grows from that tiny seed. A garden is a place where deep therapy can take place. The garden reflects back to you the areas where you need to grow and also your areas of strength. When I'm in my garden I feel peace at the core of my being. It is where I meditate and receive guidance. It is my haven. I experience great joy through its beauty and ever-changing dynamics. Co-created gardens are sanctuaries of love, the most sacred of all energies.

Re-sacralizing Partner Earth can also take place by the creation of earth art, which you can make when you work with the environment surrounding you, the available natural materials, and the Devas. It can be simple, transient, and solitary, meaning not to be viewed by others, necessarily. It is your co-creation and gift to the earth. During a devic intensive Mary co-created a beautiful piece of earth art that was a reflection of her core self, as well as a visual representation of the feminine essence of Partner Earth. She found a

Photograph by Pam Montgomery

large uprooted tree in the woods with its roots jutting up into the air and its earthen base facing the sky. Just below it was a stream. She carried water from the stream and used it to sculpt Root Woman with the dirt, rocks, and roots of the fallen tree.

On another occasion, while Brooke was teaching at my place, we divided into small groups of five people and each group co-created a piece of earth art. One group honored the Eagle and Brooke's teachings by co-creating a motif of an Eagle with leaves. It was autumn, and many different-colored leaves were available. They made a circle with old fallen grapevine and then filled the background with red leaves. The Eagle's head was made by turning red leaves over to give a whitish effect. They used yellow leaves for the beak and dark bark for the eyes. This piece of art was a magnificent representation that used the natural materials at hand and reflected the theme of the workshop.

One year, at the Women's Herbal Conference, we co-created the Goddess out of sand at the edge of a lake. We used shells and rocks for necklaces and eyes, water grass for hair, and logs for legs.

Through our earth art we honored the Goddess in each of ourselves and the Earth Goddess. We celebrated her by circling her and singing her praises. It was a playful and joyful encounter with our relatives sand, water, rock, grass, shells, and wood, as well as a communion with the deep feminine.

Andy Goldsworthy has presented his amazing pieces of earth art in a book entitled *A Collaboration with Nature*. His creations are strictly elements of nature that he is inspired to work with and that are available to him. He lives within the cycles of the seasons, making ice sculptures in winter and colored leaf displays in fall. On a daily level the weather can have a tremendous effect. A sculpture of leaves on a windy day becomes a transient piece, changing just as the Earth is changing. Because he works within the energy of place, his relationship to his art is deeply intimate and full of discovery. His intention through his work is not to alter the landscape but instead to alter perception of the elements within a landscape by inviting the intrinsic beauty of nature to emerge through skillful shaping into aesthetic form. Thus, a simple pile of leaves becomes a hanging sculpture that plays with light and wind. His innovative use of natural materials allows the viewer to look beyond the surface of the ordinary into the deeper place of essence—the place of sacred sight where the divine is glimpsed.

The next level of sacred space unfolds when the elements merge into the erotic. Terry Tempest Williams speaks of the erotics of place in her book *Desert Quartet*:

> Once I enter the Joint Trail, it is as though I am walking through the inside of an animal. It is dark, cool, and narrow with sheer sandstone walls on either side of me. I look up, a slit of sky above. Light is deceptive here. The palms of my hands search for a pulse in the rocks. I continue walking. In some places my hips can barely fit through. I turn sideways, my chest and back in a vise of geologic time. I stop. The silence that lives in these sacred hallways presses against me. I relax. I surrender. I close my eyes. The arousal of my breath rises in me like music, like love, as the possessive muscles between my legs tighten and release. I come to the rock in a moment of stillness, giving and receiving, where there is no partition between my body and the body of Earth.

Here in this place of merging, the creative life force is a continual current pulsing through the earth, through rock, through us. When we touch Partner Earth in this way, currents of passion reverberate through her, extending to all other relatives and allowing a gush of release to settle into a deep peace. Just as a sacred bond is created when two people experience orgasm together, so is sacred space created when this level of intimacy is reached with Partner Earth. Do we dare give ourselves permission to love Partner Earth and all our relations in such an erotic way? Perhaps part of our evolution is taking the erotic out of the realm of debasement and bringing it into the realm of the sacred.

8

EXERCISES TO ENHANCE PARTNERING

EXCHANGE OF BREATH
WITH THE GREEN WORLD

Close your eyes and begin taking deep breaths. Breathe slowly into your toes and fingertips, your legs and arms. Take another deep breath and breathe into your back and chest, slowly. Now, breathe into your shoulders and neck. Breathe deeply into your head and feel how relaxed you are. Breathe, now, into all your internal organs and feel the oxygen being carried by your blood to every cell of your being, reviving and nourishing you. Breathe slowly, now, and as you breathe feel the deep nourishment you receive from this life-giving breath. As you breathe, notice the green world around you. Picture in your mind's eye the leaves of trees, the plants and grasses, the flowers and bushes. As you breathe, notice the green world and its breath. Together with your green relatives, inhale and exhale. As you breathe, filling your cells with oxygen, that life-giving element, you notice a cycle of breath between you and the green beings. Inhale, exhale. As you inhale oxygen your green relatives exhale oxygen, and as you exhale carbon dioxide the green ones inhale carbon dioxide in a cycle of breath with the green world. Breathe slowly, now, and as you breathe feel the green breath of the plants as you inhale. Exhaling, feel how the trees take in your breath. In-breath is the green beings' exhalation, out-breath is the green beings' inhalation. Cycle your breath with your green relatives. In your mind's eye, see the circle of breath with the green world. Feel how this green breath nourishes you at the core of your being. This exchange of breath with the green ones is constant. Every second of every minute of every hour of every day, the cycle of breath goes on with the green world. Without your green relatives you would not have the life-giving oxygen, and without your carbon dioxide your green relatives would not have their life-giving element. There is an equal exchange, equal partnership by this sharing of breath together. Now, breathe deeply and feel the deep intimate communion that takes place between you and the green world through your breath. Each day as you walk out the door, greet the green beings with a conscious exchange of breath, and be grateful for them in your life. (This exercise was originally inspired by Susun Weed.)

PLANT ALLY

Plant allies are green beings that are here to aid in your particular growth and/or health process at this particular time, either for a long time or for a short time in an acute or crisis situation. Plant allies usually grow near you or are in your life in some way or another without your even realizing it. For example, if you don't live where you have an outdoor environment to be with the plants, perhaps you bring cut flowers into your home and you have a particular attraction to roses. Roses are serving as your ally. When you move into conscious partnership with your plant ally, much healing can take place.

To discover which plant is your ally, pay attention to the plants you are attracted to. Pay attention to the plant coming out of the crack in the sidewalk outside your apartment. Particularly pay attention to the plant in the sidewalk crack where you trip or stub your toe. You may work with a plant ally on all levels of your being: physical, emotional, mental, and spiritual. If you're not aware of your plant ally, you can visit the Wise One within to discover your plant ally. The following is a meditation to help introduce you to your plant ally.

Close your eyes and imagine yourself at the top of a golden spiral staircase. Begin to descend the staircase, one step at a time. As you step down, you feel the radiance emanating from the staircase. Golden rays of light surround you as you go down, further and further down the spiral staircase. You notice the staircase is coming to an end in what appears to be a large cavern. Down, ever deeper, you descend into the heart of your being. You step off the staircase into a softly lit cave deep in Partner Earth. You notice that the walls glitter with crystals. As you slowly take in the expanse of this great cavern you notice a woman sitting on a rock on the far side of the cave. She beckons to you. As you approach, you feel as if you know her from somewhere. She speaks to you when you've reached her side: "Dear One, it's so nice to see you again. I have a gift for you. Please come sit with me so that I may give you this most precious gift." You sit beside her, feeling completely comfortable and at home. You are totally relaxed in her presence. She says, "Dear One, receive not only with your hands but also with your heart this plant ally I have to give to you." You stretch out your hands and open your heart, and she places your plant ally in your hands. You observe every detail of your ally: its color, its shape, its size, its smell, its texture, and its aura. The Wise Woman tells you, "This ally has much to teach you. You can grow and heal with this plant. Listen to what it has to share with you." Take time, now, to listen to your ally. Listen with your heart and you will receive deep understanding. When you have finished, you may return to your waking reality by going back the way you came.

Sometimes, after doing this meditation, people still are not sure what their plant ally is. Usually within a short period of time it becomes apparent, as Rita's story shows. After the visualization in the cave, Rita still didn't recognize her plant ally. However, she did notice that the leaves were in clusters of threes. The next morning she came out of her apartment and saw from the corner of her eye a rose branch that had clusters of three leaves. That same day, Rita was looking in the book *Spiritual Properties of Herbs,* and saw there a drawing of the stages of human consciousness, represented on branches with clusters of three leaves. To Rita they represented the maiden, mother, and crone—the full feminine consciousness. To others they may represent the Father, Son, and Holy Spirit, and to still others they may represent body, mind, and spirit. The next day while walking down the street in New York City, Rita found on the sidewalk a long-stemmed red rose with its cluster of three leaves intact. This was her third encounter over three days with three leaves. Rita knew then that the rose was her plant ally. As her ally, the rose helps her to open her heart chakra. Rita says, "The rose unfolds the way consciousness does, in layers. It represents many layers of love, friendship, romance, and the collective. Through its representation of the trinity, it brings me to a deeper understanding of my feminine aspect." The rose has served Rita in many ways over the past few years. It has softened her and helped her to be more compassionate. It has healed her heart and brought her to the deep feminine. It has become a life-long friend and ally.

SOUND RESONANCE

Sound is one of the best avenues for opening lines of communication with other relatives. Sound is universal and can be understood in all dimensions and by all beings. Sound waves can be ridden like horses and take you to places far and wide. You can follow sound to the depths of your being as if journeying to the center of Partner Earth or to the farthest star. Different sounds create different frequencies. Every plant, rock, animal, tree, stream, river, ocean, star, and cloud carries a particular frequency. Artificially made objects carry frequency, as well. Anything with a molecular structure that vibrates carries a frequency. People have known for eons that sound can produce altered states and that through sound, avenues of communication become open.

The most common uses of sound are the shamanic technique of drumming to create an opening, and the chanting used in various cultures and religions across the planet. Sound is now being used to help balance the right and left sides of the brain, as well as to heal degenerative disease. Toning is another use of sound that I have found to be helpful in partnering with my relatives. Each chakra (energy center) has a particular tone that helps open that center. The root chakra has the sound of oo-oo-oo, the hara has the sound of oh-h-h, the solar plexus has the sound of aw-w-w, the heart has the sound of ah-h-h, the throat has the sound of ih-h-h, the third eye has the sound of eh-h-h, and the crown has the sound of e-e-e. Usually, one of these tones will open a doorway to communicating with one of your relatives. If you're not sure where to begin, the heart chakra is a good place. When you open your heart by toning "ah-h-h," a softening takes place and barriers fall away. As you refine your ability to communicate, other tones and sounds will feel more appropriate to you. Stay alert to your intuition about which tone or sound resonance to use to partner with relatives. Musical instruments can also create openings. I have found drums, rattles, wind pipes, bells, and crystal bowls to be of particular assistance. Of course, the universal tone is that of *Om*. This is the sound the galaxies make as they whirl through space.

Practice sound resonance by picking a relative that you have a hard time communicating with, perhaps a particular plant or animal or even a room in your house or your car. Begin by toning "ah-h-h" to open your heart to this relative that you have not always viewed as a friend. Do this for some time until you begin to move away from judgment and into the one heart space. As you soften, begin to see the beauty in this relative. Ask what frequency this particular relative operates on, and then listen. Let go of control, put aside the "nag," and let sound emerge. Perhaps you'll have the urge to sing, chant, tone, or play an instrument. Do whatever you are moved to do. Resonate with your relative for a good amount of time. Allow the walls to crumble, let the fortress of defense melt away. Defense serves no one. Ask to be in service to the highest good of all. When it feels as if you are on the same wave length, ask what you can do to bring balance in this partnership. It's important to have clear intentions. Listen again with your whole being. After you have received guidance, be sure to thank your relative and then act on whatever guidance you received. You may return to communicate with this relative at any time by resonating on the same frequency again.

LISTEN TO RELATIVES

Listening to your relatives is a form of meditation. It involves quieting the inner chatter in order to hear what your relatives have to say. I begin by visualizing the water surface of a pond. I watch the ripples and one by one let them settle until the water is smooth. I follow my breath slowly through my body, relaxing each muscle as I go. As I breathe deeper, I become calmer and quieter. I take my ego self and set it aside so that I may hear without judgment. I let go of controlling the situation, trusting that the outcome or guidance is exactly what is needed to bring balance at this particular time. I then ask to be connected to the Deva of whatever it is I'm concerned with that day. Asking is a very important part of the process. We must choose to be in partnership. I then ask for guidance, for something specific, something broad, depending on the situation. I listen with "big ears," which means that I listen with my whole body, not just my mind. I pay attention to every little detail and nuance. Keen observation is a key to good communication. My body response tells me the most. I look for a felt sense and then give it a handle: a word or image that helps me recall it later. Sometimes I experience something like a daydream, which is a scenario playing out in my mind. Watching the play and feeling my participation at the same time, I am both the observer and the observed. I notice every impression that is left on my being. Almost always there is some type of action to be taken from the guidance I receive. Remember, this is about manifestation. As I mentioned earlier, the quality of your partnering is directly related to how willing you are to act upon your impressions. It is the action I take that creates the partnership. Otherwise, I am engaged in idle information gathering that serves no purpose. When I end my listening session, I always thank Lumelligence for the gift of our partnership.

DNA ALIGNMENT MEDITATION

This meditation follows the progression of Moon Flower Essences that you will find in Table 1 on page 84. Each flower is visualized along with the corresponding associations that aid in the process of realigning fragmented DNA strands. This meditation can be added to as you deepen your work with realignment of light filaments.

Close your eyes and begin to breathe slowly. Allow your breath to warm and massage every cell of your being, becoming more and more relaxed with each breath. As you breathe see the color red at the base of your spine swirling like a vortex in your root chakra. Breathe into this swirling red light and visualize all the pieces of red light coming together. As you breathe hear the oo-oo-oo sound rising from your root chakra. Make this sound. As you tone visualize spirals of red light moving through your bones and muscles, gathering fragments of light, re-membering the light. As you breathe spirals of red light all of the human-made inanimate form comes into balance in this spiral of red light. You move into oneness with these forms, knowing them as yourself and partnering with your relatives. Breathe, now, and as you breathe let the spiral of red light ground you into the earth. Feel the solidness of the earth under you, knowing that this ground wire is essential to the flow of energy. Breathe, now, and bring into the spiral of red light the remaining fragments that are needed to complete the strand of red light. Now visualize the Mexican Sunflower, known as Tithonia Torch, and place this flower in the center of the spiraling vortex of red light. Feel how the essence of Tithonia Torch brings all the fragments of light into wholeness.

As you breathe see the color orange in your belly swirling like a vortex of orange light in your hara chakra. Breathe into the swirling orange light and visualize all pieces of orange light coming together. As you breathe hear the oh-h-h sound rising from your hara. Make this sound. As you tone visualize spirals of orange light moving through your reproductive system gathering fragments of light, re-membering the light. As you breathe spirals of orange light all natural inanimate form comes into balance in the spiral of orange light. You move into oneness with these forms, knowing them as yourself and partnering with natural inanimate form. Breathe, now, and as you breathe let the spiral of orange light release old patterns, knowing that what no longer serves you does not serve the highest good. Breathe, now, and bring into the spiral of orange light the remaining fragments that are needed to complete the strand of orange light. Now visualize the Sunflower and place this flower in the center of the spiraling vortex of orange light. Feel how the essence of Sunflower brings all the fragments of light into wholeness.

As you breathe see the color yellow in your stomach, swirling like a vortex in your solar plexus chakra. Breathe into the swirling yellow light and visualize all pieces of yellow light coming together. As you breathe, hear the aw-w-w sound rising from your solar plexus chakra. Make this sound. As you tone visualize spirals of yellow light moving through your digestive system, gathering fragments of light, re-membering the light. As you breathe spirals of yellow light, the element water comes into balance in the spiral of yellow light. You move into oneness with water, knowing water as yourself, partnering with water. Breathe, now, and as you breathe let the spiral of yellow light move you into trust, knowing that when you trust you are placing yourself in the vast web of interconnected relations where each affects the other. Breathe, now, and bring into the spiral of yellow light the remaining fragments that are needed to complete the strand of yellow light. Now visualize Borage and place this flower in the center of the spiraling vortex of yellow light. Feel how the essence of Borage brings all the fragments of light into wholeness.

As you breathe see the color green in your heart, swirling like a vortex in your heart chakra. Breathe into the swirling green light and visualize all pieces of green light coming together. As you breathe, hear the ah-h-h sound rising from your heart chakra. Make this sound. As you tone visualize spirals of green light moving through your circulatory system gathering fragments of light, re-membering the light. As you breathe spirals of green light, the element of earth comes into balance in the spiral of green light. You move into oneness with earth, knowing her as yourself, partnering with earth. Breathe, now, and as you breathe let the spiral green light bring joy to you in your daily life, knowing that joy brings bliss, which is the bridge between spirit and form. Breathe, now, and bring into the spiral of green light the remaining fragments that are needed to complete the strand of green light. Now visualize Lavender and place this flower in the center of the spiraling vortex of green light. Feel how the essence of Lavender brings all the fragments of light into wholeness.

As you breathe see the color blue in your throat swirling like a vortex in your throat chakra. Breathe into the swirling blue light and visualize all pieces of blue light coming together. As you breathe hear the sound ih-h-h rising from your throat chakra. Make this sound. As you tone visualize spirals of blue light moving through your respiratory system, gathering fragments of light, re-membering the light. As you breathe spirals of blue light, the element of air comes into balance in the spiral of blue light. You move into oneness with air, knowing it as yourself, partnering with air. Breathe, now, and as you breathe let the spiral of blue light move you into compassion, knowing that compassion is the doorway to the heart and the deep understanding that we all are divine beings. Breathe, now, and bring into the spiral of blue light the remaining fragments that are needed to complete the strand of blue light. Now visualize Heart's Ease and place this flower in the center of the spiraling vortex of blue light. Feel how the essence of Heart's Ease brings all the fragments of light into wholeness.

As you breathe see the color indigo between your eyes, swirling like a vortex in your Third Eye chakra. Breathe into this swirling indigo light and visualize all pieces of indigo light coming together. As you breathe hear the eh-h-h sound rising from your third eye chakra. Make this sound. As you tone visualize spirals of indigo light moving through your immune system, gathering fragments of light, re-membering the light. As you breathe spirals of indigo light, the sun and the element of fire come into balance in the spiral of indigo light. You move into oneness with sun and fire, knowing them as yourself, partnering with sun and fire. Breathe, now, and as you breathe let the spiral of indigo light help you to love yourself, knowing that you must love yourself before you can truly love any other relation. Breathe, now, and bring into the spiral of indigo light the remaining fragments that are needed to complete the strand of indigo light. Now visualize Calendula and place this flower in the center of the spiraling vortex of indigo light. Feel how the essence of Calendula brings all the fragments of light into the wholeness.

As you breathe see the color purple at the top of your head, swirling like a vortex in your crown chakra. Breathe into the swirling purple light and visualize all pieces of purple light coming together. As you breathe hear the e-e-e sound rising from your crown chakra. Make this sound. As you tone visualize spirals of purple light moving through your nervous system, gathering fragments of light, re-membering the light. As you breathe spirals of purple light, the moon comes into balance in the spiral of purple light. You move into oneness with the moon, knowing her as yourself, partnering with the moon. Breathe, now, and as you breathe let the spiral of purple light bring your attention *to synchronicity knowing that synchronicity is Lumelligence knocking at the door and that when we pay attention to it we invite spirit in. Breathe, now, and bring into the spiral of purple light the remaining fragments that are needed to complete the strand of purple light. Now visualize Loosestrife and place this flower in the center of the spiraling vortex of purple light. Feel how the essence of Loosestrife brings all the fragments of light into wholeness.*

As you breathe see the color pink just above your head, swirling like a vortex in your astral chakra. Breathe into the swirling pink light and visualize all pieces of pink light coming together. As you breathe hear the sound of the drum. Make this sound. As you drum visualize spirals of pink light moving through your emotional being and bringing stability as fragments of light are gathered and light is re-membered. As you breathe spirals of pink light, all of the minerals, stones, and rocks come into balance in the spiral of pink light. You move into oneness with these relatives, knowing them as yourself, partnering with minerals, stones, and rocks. Breathe, now, and as you breathe let the spiral of pink light help you to give and receive energy, knowing that exchange of energy is the vehicle that moves the life force. When we share energy we engage with life. Breathe, now, and bring into the spiral of pink light the remaining fragments that are needed to complete the strand of pink light. Now visualize Hyssop and place this flower in the center of the spiraling vortex of pink light. Feel how the essence of Hyssop brings all the fragments of light into wholeness.

As you breathe, see the color pastel yellow a little further above your head, swirling like a vortex in your ethereal chakra. Breathe into the swirling light and visualize all pieces of pastel yellow light coming together. As you breathe hear the sound of the wind pipe rising from your ethereal chakra. Make this sound. As you play the wind pipe, visualize spirals of pastel yellow light moving through your mental being, bringing clarity as fragments of light are gathered and the light is re-membered. As you breathe spirals of pastel yellow light, all of the plants and trees come into balance in the spiral of pastel yellow light. You move into oneness with plants and trees, knowing them as yourself, partnering with plants and trees. Breathe, now, and as you breathe let the spiral of pastel yellow light help you to stay in the evolutionary energy flow, knowing that your life will run smoothly if you follow this path of least resistance. Breathe, now, and bring into the spiral of pastel yellow light the remaining fragments that are needed to complete the strand of pastel yellow light. Now visualize Morning Glory and place this flower in the center of the spiraling vortex of pastel yellow light. Feel how the essence of Morning Glory brings all the fragments of light into wholeness.

As you breathe, see the color lime green a few feet above your head, swirling like a vortex in your transcendent chakra. Breathe into this swirling lime-green light and visualize all pieces of lime-green light coming together. As you breathe hear the sound of a rattle rising from your transcendent chakra. Make this sound. As you rattle visualize spirals of lime-green light moving through your spiritual being, bringing awareness as you gather fragments of light, re-membering the light. As you breathe spirals of lime-green light, all of the animals come into balance in the spiral of lime-green light. You move into oneness with animals, knowing them as yourself, partnering with animals. Breathe, now, and as you breathe let the spiral of lime-green light open you to receiving guidance, knowing that allowing this help from the spirit world brings balance and peace. Breathe, now, and bring into the spiral of lime-green light the remaining fragments that are needed to complete the strand of lime-green light. Now visualize Cosmos and place this flower in the center of the spiraling vortex of lime-green light. Feel how the essence of Cosmos brings all the fragments of light into the wholeness.

As you breathe, see the color sky blue as far away as the planets and yet still connected to you, swirling like a vortex in your planetary chakra. Breathe into the swirling sky-blue light and visualize all pieces of sky-blue light coming together. As you breathe hear the sound of bells rising from your planetary chakra. Make this sound. As you ring a bell visualize spirals of sky-blue light moving through your earth body, feeling the essence of you as earth, gathering fragments of light, re-membering the light. As you breathe spirals of sky-blue light, all humans come into balance in the spiral of sky-blue light. You move into oneness with other humans knowing them as yourself, partnering with humans. Breathe, now, and as you breathe let the spiral of sky-blue light help you touch into source energy, knowing that this revitalizes and nourishes you at the deepest level. Breathe, now, and bring into the spiral of sky-blue light the remaining fragments that are needed to complete the strand of sky-blue light. Now visualize Purple Coneflower and place this flower in the center of the spiraling vortex of sky-blue light. Feel how the essence of Purple Coneflower brings all the fragments of light into the wholeness.

As you breathe see the color lavender as far away as the universe but still connected to you, swirling like a vortex in your universal chakra. Breathe into this swirling lavender light and visualize all pieces of lavender light coming together. As you breathe hear the sound of crystal resonance rising from your universal chakra. Make this sound. As you play the crystal bowl visualize spirals of lavender light moving through your soul, sensing its path as you gather fragments of light, re-membering the light. As you breathe spirals of lavender light, all conceptual thought form comes into balance in the spiral of lavender light. You move into oneness with conceptual thought form, knowing it as yourself, partnering with conceptual thought form, Breathe, now, and as you breathe let the spiral of lavender light bring you into partnering with all of life, knowing that here is where true evolution takes place. Breathe, now, and bring into the spiral of lavender light the remaining fragments that are needed to complete the strand of lavender light. Now visualize Foxglove and place this flower in the center of the spiraling vortex of lavender light. Feel how the essence of Foxglove brings all the fragments of light into wholeness.

As you breathe, see all the strands of light—red, orange, yellow, green, blue, indigo, purple, pink, pastel yellow, lime-green, sky-blue, and lavender—spiraling together up through all your chakras: spiraling in perfect alignment, completely whole. As you breathe visualize all the strands together making a pillar of spiraling light that becomes white light. As you breathe sound the tone of Om, the cosmic tone. Visualize this pillar of white light connecting your cosmic consciousness to creator. As you breathe, visualizing all the strands of DNA aligned in the oneness of white light, see yourself aligned to the cosmos, partnering with the cosmos. Breathe, now, and as you breathe let the pillar of white light bring balanced and harmonized energy, knowing that this is your connection to the divine. Now visualize Butterfly Bush and place this flower in the white light vortex of the creator chakra. Feel the essence of Butterfly Bush bringing fullness and wholeness to *your being. Breathe into this pillar of crystalline white light that holds all other strands of light, and know the divine truth of your being. And, now, as you bring your breath back to a regular rhythm, feel the light essence of your being. Let the light shine through.*

"I Am" Visualization

This visualization is from the Fairy Messages® put out by Baker & Peterson (see the Resources section): individual cards with messages on them. (I've written "I am" rather than "You are," and the last affirmation is my own). I find them to be inspiring and helpful in moving into the oneness with all our relatives.

I am the flames of a bonfire stretching to meet the stars.
I am a dolphin surfing in the shimmering sea.
I am the rushing waters of a river that never stops.
I am the sweet breath of a pine forest.
I am the gentle hush of falling snow.
I am the silent flight of the owl swooping through the night.
I am the rustle of wind sweeping through the trees.
I am a red-tailed hawk chasing the wind.
I am the sparkle of an ice storm.
I am the laughing pebble tumbling in the stream.
I am the stealth of a tiger prowling through the jungle.
I am the clean smell of rain on a hot summer afternoon.
I am a bee sipping the nectar from a honeysuckle.
I am the never-melting snow on the highest mountain peak.
I am a baby bird flying for the first time.
I am the warm wind whispering secrets.
I am a jewel hidden in an ancient stone.
I am the rush of golden leaves falling from the trees.
I am the silence of the cave where the black bear lies.
I am the strength of a giant redwood.
I am the safe warmth of a caterpillar's cocoon.
I am the delicate perfume of spring flowers.
I am the spark that becomes a dancing flame.

I am the roaring thunder of an erupting volcano.
I am the last flashing light of a fading sunset.
I am the many eyes of a peacock's tail feathers.
I am the brightness of the moon lighting up the darkness.
I am the watchfulness of a crocodile floating in the river.
I am a singing cricket welcoming the night.
I am the sweet burst of freshly picked blackberries.
I am a butterfly dancing over a sunlit field.
I am a rainbow in a crystal.
I am an icicle hanging from a mountain ledge.
I am the morning light as it first touches the earth.
I am the glistening diamonds caught on a spider's web.
I am the lightning bolt flashing through the clouds.
I am the bending grass cradling the morning dew.
I am the fluttering tips of palm leaves tickling the sky.
I am the greenness of a meadow in spring.
I am the colored glass rubbed smooth by the ocean waves.
I am a dinosaur's footprint resting in a rock.
I am the shadows weaving themselves in the depths of the forest.
I am the echo of a wolf's howl.
I am the dandelion's puff of seeds floating in the air.
I am the first star of night twinkling and winking.
I am the bright orange of pumpkins growing in a field.
I am the cool breeze signaling autumn.
I am the drumming of raindrops falling from a blackened sky.
I am a fragrant orange blossom open to the sun.
I am a swiftly moving leaf rafting down the river.
I am the quiet pond listening to the frog's evening songs.
I am the patience of a tiny seed waiting beneath the snow.
I am the rainbow mist of a waterfall.

and inspired by the Fairy Messages®, I created my own affirmation:

I am a uniquely divine being who weaves myself into the vast web of
interconnected oneness.

CREATING CEREMONY

Ceremony is a conscious act of connecting to the vast web of life. It can be formalized with previously prescribed actions and repeated at various times, yet I find the most meaningful ceremony is one that is spontaneous and/or is created by the participants. It is a way to partner with all of life and to give thanks to all your relatives for their part in the connection with all of life. It is also a time of communion—common-union—coming together as a family. In creating ceremony, do what speaks to you, what moves you, what inspires you, what excites you. You may want to set up an altar with items that are meaningful to you and your group. It is usually nice to place a personal item on the altar that you want to infuse with the energy of the ceremony. I like to call in the seven directions to add their spirits to the circle. You may also want to include others, like your ancestors, certain animals, or other relatives. Ceremony can incorporate the elements of fire, air, water, and earth in any way.

A talking stick is often used in ceremony. This is any object that has been designated for the purpose of talking and listening. The talking stick is passed among the group, and the person holding it is the only one who speaks. This person's responsibility in holding the stick is to speak truth from the heart. Everyone else's responsibility is to listen with the heart. You may want to either focus the talking stick on a particular subject or leave it up to whatever spontaneously arises from each person. There also may be a time for intentional prayer as a group and/or a time to listen to what your relatives have to offer to the ceremony.

Of course, ceremony is also about celebration, so you want to incorporate singing, dancing, and making music. Don't forget that this process of en-lightening is a joyful one. We have a tendency to get very serious about connecting with spirit—keep it light. Let your imagination be free to create a dynamic mandala that serves all our relations.

Appendix

How to Make Flower Essences

There are several different ways to make flower essences, and all of them are good. It's important that you pay attention to the method that speaks to you. I will share with you the way I make essences in the hope that you will stay open to your own guidance and inspiration.

The ingredients are simple: light, flowers, water, open heart, and clear mind. To make essences with sunlight it is ideal to have full sun, but on a somewhat cloudy day you can still make them. Flower essences made in moonlight are best made during the three-day period before, during, and after the full moon when there are not too many clouds. Sun essences need at least two full hours of bright sunlight. If it's cloudy they will need to be in the sun for four to six hours. Moon essences can be put out when it gets dark, and left out overnight, and brought in at or before dawn.

Begin by sitting quietly with the flower that you are attracted to. Ask to be connected to the Lumelligence of this flower. Put out your intention clearly that you want to use the essence of this flower for healing purposes and you would like guidance in how best to do that. Let the Deva of the flower know that you would like to understand how to use this essence for yourself and other relatives. Then take time to listen to what you receive. Listen not only with your ears but with your whole body. Pay attention to everything, no matter how small it may seem.

When you feel that you have received all you need from the Deva of the flower, ask which blossoms want to become essence. They let you know in innumerable ways which blossom to choose; for example, one may nod in the breeze or turn toward you, or one's color will be more radiant than another's. Put a leaf from the plant between your thumb and forefinger and pick the blossoms that want to become essence. I don't touch the flowers because I like them to remain as pure in their own essential energy as possible. Put these blossoms in a small clear glass bowl filled with spring water. I like to cover the top of the water with flowers because I love the appearance of the flowers floating in the water. Place the bowl where it can get maximum light and will not be disturbed by animals. (Dogs and cats love flower essences on hot summer days.)

After the essence has been in the light for the necessary amount of time, make your essence preparation by preserving the essence with brandy and diluting it. The theory behind dilution is that less is more. The more dilute the energetic essence of a plant is, the more potent it becomes. Take an amber bottle and fill it half full of potentized water (the water that the flowers were floating in) and the other half with brandy. This is called the mother essence. Next take a one-ounce amber bottle and fill it half with spring water and half with brandy and ten drops from the mother essence. This is called the stock bottle. From this, you can make dosage bottles by filling a half-ounce amber bottle with two-thirds spring water, one-third brandy, and ten drops from the stock. At this point, many people like to potentize the essence by shaking it or hitting it on the palm of the hand a hundred times. I find this unnecessary because the essences are already potent enough.

An average dosage of flower essence is four drops under the tongue as needed. I think it is best to use kinesiology to check for dosage and the number of times a day to take an essence. If you have stock bottles and don't want to make dosage bottles, you can put four drops from the stock bottle into a half cup of water and drink it.

Be sure to label the bottle with the name of the flower; whether it is the mother essence, stock, or dosage bottle; the date; and any other pertinent information such as "full moon in Leo" or "solar eclipse." Your essence is now ready to be used for yourself, friends, family, clients, and other relatives.

BIBLIOGRAPHY

Adams, Patch, *Gesundheit*. Rochester, VT: Healing Arts Press, 1993.

Baker, Melissa, and Peterson, Kila Staub, *Fairy Messages*. Sebastopol, CA: Baker & Peterson, 1993.

Bloom, William, *Devas, Fairies, and Angels*. Glastonbury, UK: Gothic Image Publications, 1986.

Buchbinder, Hayley. Talking Trash. *The Sciences*, Vol. 35, No. 3, May/June 1995, pp. 8–9.

Chopra, Deepak, *Quantum Healing*. New York: Bantam Books, 1989.

Dawson, Adele, *Herbs, Partners in Life, A Guide to Cooking, Gardening, and Healing With Wild and Cultivated Plants*. Rochester, VT: Healing Arts Press, 1991.

Devereux, Paul, *Earthmind*. Rochester, VT: Destiny Books, 1989.

Ellsworth, Paul, *Direct Healing*. North Hollywood, CA: Newcastle, 1982.

Gaskell, G.A., *Dictionary of All Scriptures and Myths*. New York: Random House, 1993.

Gendlin, Eugene, *Focusing*. New York: Bantam Books, 1981.

Gibbs, Nancy, *Angels Among Us*. Time, Vol. 142, No. 27, December 27, 1993, pp. 56–65.

Gladstar, Rosemary, *Natural Cosmetics and Skin Care*. East Barre, VT: Sage (802-479-9825).

Goldsworthy, Andy, *A Collaboration with Nature*. New York: Harry Abrams, 1990.

Gore, Al, *Earth in the Balance: Ecology and the Human Spirit*. New York: Plume Penguin Books, 1993.

Green, Lorna, *Earth Age, A New Vision of God, the Human, and the Earth*. New York: Paulist Press, 1994.

Licata, Vincent, *Comfrey and Chlorophyll*. Santa Ana, CA: Continental Health Research, 1971.

Longren, Sig, *The Pendulum Kit*. New York: Simon & Schuster, 1990.

Maclean, Dorothy, *To Hear the Angels Sing*. Elgin, IL: Lorian Press, 1980.

Nearing, Helen and Scott, *Living the Good Life*. New York: Schocken Books, 1970.

Petranek, Stephen, The Force of Nature. *Life,* September 1993, pp. 30–37.

Redfield, James, *The Celestine Prophecy*. New York: Time Warner, 1993.

Sams, Jamie, *Sacred Path Cards*. New York: HarperCollins, 1990.

Small Wright, Machaelle, *Behaving As If the God in All Life Mattered*. Warrenton, VA: Perelandra, 1987.

————, Workbook Workshop. Warrenton, VA: Perelandra Tape Series 7, 1990.

Tellington-Jones, Linda, and Taylor, Sybil, *The Tellington Touch*. New York: Viking Penguin, 1992.

Tempest Williams, Terry, *An Unspoken Hunger*. New York: Vintage Books, 1994.

————, *Desert Quartet*. New York: Pantheon Books, 1995.

Zukav, Gary, *Seat of the Soul*. New York: Simon & Schuster, 1990.

Resources

Books

Cowan, Eliot, *Plant Spirit Medicine*. Newberg, OR: Swan Raven Co., 1995.

Macy, Joanna, *World As Lover, World As Self*. Berkeley, CA: Parallax Press, 1991.

Marciniak, Barbara, *Bringers of the Dawn & Earth; Pleiadian Keys to the Living Library*. Santa Fe, NM: Bear & Co., 1995.

Medicine Eagle, Brooke, *Buffalo Woman Comes Singing*. New York: Ballantine Books, 1991.

Noble, Vicki, *Shakti Woman*. San Francisco: Harper, 1991.

Roads, Michael, *Talking with Nature, Journey into Nature, Journey into Oneness*. Tiburon, CA: H. J. Kramer, 1994.

Seed, John, et al., *Thinking Like A Mountain: Toward a Council of All Beings*. Philadelphia, PA: New Society Publishers, 1988.

Sheldrake, Rupert, *The Rebirth of Nature*. Rochester, VT: Park Street Press, 1994.

Small Wright, Machaelle, *Perelandra Garden Workbook*. Warrenton, VA: Perelandra, 1987.

Talbot, Michael, *The Holographic Universe*. New York: HarperCollins, 1991.

FLOWER ESSENCES

Perelandra Flower Essences
Center for Nature Research
P.O. Box 3603
Warrenton, VA 22186

Woodland Essence
Box 206
Cold Brook, NY 13324

Green Hope Flower Essences
P.O. Box 125
Meriden, NH 03770

Flower Essence Society
P.O. Box 459
Nevada City, CA 95959

Green Terrestrial
P.O. Box 266
Milton, NY 12547

Flower Vision Research
244 Madison Ave.
Suite 6H
New York, NY 10016

Alaskan Flower Essence Project
Box 1369
Homer, AK 99603

Flowers of the Soul
Town Highway 8, 117C
West Danville, VT 05873

Running Fox Farm Flower Essences
P.O. Box 381
Worthington, MA 01098

FLOWER ESSENCE PRACTITIONERS

Gail Ulrich
P.O. Box 6
Shelburne Falls, MA 01370

Hart Brent
Town Highway 8
117C, West Danville, VT 05873

Mary Dudek
R.R. 1
Box 240A, Elizaville, NY 12523

DEVIC GARDENS

Green Terrestrial
P.O. Box 266
Milton, NY 12547

Avena Botanicals
20 Mill Street
Rockland, ME 04841

Perelandra
P.O. Box 3606
Warrenton, VA 22186

WORKSHOPS

Green Terrestrial
P.O. Box 266
Milton, NY 12547

Woodland Essence
Box 206
Cold Brook, NY 13324

Ocean Mammal Institute
P.O. Box 14422
Reading, PA 19612

Avena Botanicals
20 Mill Street
Rockland, ME 04841

Blazing Star Herbal School
P.O. Box 6
Shelburne Falls, MA 01370

Wise Woman Center
P.O. Box 69
Woodstock, NY 12498

Sage Mountain
Box 420
East Barre, VT 05649

Singing Eagle Enterprises
No. 1 2nd Avenue East
C401, Polson, MT 59860

Grace Spiritual Growth Training Program
Box 449A Route 28A
West Hurley, NY 12491

RETREAT CENTER

Phoenicia Pathwork Center
P.O. Box 66
Phoenicia, NY 12464

Rowe Conference Center
King's Highway Road
Rowe, MA 01367

Blacktail Ranch
Wolf Creek, MT 59648

ORGANIZATIONS

United Plant Savers
Box 420
East Barre, VT 05649

Partner Earth Education Center
P.O. Box 266
Milton, NY 12547

Institute for Deep Ecology
P.O. Box 1050
Occidental, CA 95465

OTHER

Angel Cards
Drake & Taylor
order from:
Music Design Inc.
46-50 Northport Washington Road
Milwaukee, WI 53212-1062

Fairy Messages®
Baker & Peterson
P.O. Box 428
Sebastopol, CA 95473
Phone: (800) 829-8183/(707) 829-8183
Fax: (707) 829-2127
E-mail: bpmessages@aol.com
Website: www.intouchmag.com/baker&peterson
Creator of five different affirmation decks for all ages.

Medicine Cards
Jamie Sams & David Carson
Bear & Co.
P.O. Drawer 2860
Santa Fe, NM 87504

Sacred Path Cards
Jamie Sams
HarperCollins
10 East 53rd Street
New York, NY 10022